Praise for *What Doesn't Kill You Makes You Stronger*

"This book is a must-read or a must-give if you or someone you know is dealing with loss."
—*Sacramento Bee*

"This is a really valuable book for anyone whose life feels as though it is coming apart. Rooted firmly in Maxine Schnall's own experience and enriched by the examples of the other people she has worked with, *What Doesn't Kill You* tells you not only how to survive loss but also how to find meaning in it."
—William Bridges, author of *Transitions* and *Managing Transitions*

"Ninety percent of the greatest things that ever happened to me were the result of smashing defeats. This book has hundreds of true stories about survival. It is a must read."
—Phyllis Diller

"A must-read for anyone in crisis. Rather than offer platitudes, Schnall gives us real life examples of people who have used tragedy to turn their lives around. Her inclusiveness and attitude of sharing experiences rather than pretending to have a universal solution for anyone who is grieving makes this book work from the very beginning."
—Cheryl Dellasega, author of *Surviving Ophelia*

"I wish I had the opportunity to read *What Doesn't Kill You Makes You Stronger* three years ago following my motorcycle accident . . . it would have been great-tasting medicine."
—Pat Croce, author of *I Feel Great, and You Will Too!* and *110%: 110 Strategies for Feeling Great Every Day*

"Maxine Schnall has written a much-needed book—especially for these difficult times. By sharing her profound wisdom with us—as well as her personal story and those of others—she shows us that we truly can find surprising gifts in any misfortune. I highly recommend it to anyone who is in crisis or has experienced a loss of any kind."
—Beverly Engel, author of *The Power of Apology: Healing Steps to Transform All Your Relationships*

Also by Maxine Schnall

My Husband, the Doctor

The Broadbelters

Your Marriage

The Wives Self Help Program

Limits: A Search for New Values

Every Woman Can Be Adored

MAXINE SCHNALL

what doesn't kill you makes you stronger

Turning Bad Breaks Into Blessings

DA CAPO PRESS
A Member of the Perseus Books Group

Designed by Reginald Thompson
Set in 11-point Sabon by The Perseus Books Group

Cataloging-in-Publication data for this book is available from the Library
of Congress.

First paperback printing October 2003
ISBN 0-7382-0860-4

Published by Da Capo Press
A Member of the Perseus Books Group
http://www.dacapopress.com

Da Capo Press books are available at special discounts for bulk purchases
in the U.S. by corporations, institutions, and other organizations. For more
information, please contact the Special Markets Department at the Perseus
Books Group, 11 Cambridge Center, Cambridge, MA 02142, or call (800)
255–1514 or (617) 252–5298, or e-mail j.mccrary@perseusbooks.com.

1   2   3   4   5   6   7   8   9—07   06   05   04   03

*For their beautiful gifts of love and loyalty
and for making me immensely proud of them,
I dedicate this book to my children,
Ilene and Rona.*

I was always looking outside myself
for strength and confidence,
but it comes from within.
It is there all the time.
Anna Freud

Contents

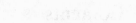

Acknowledgments

Writing a book can be a very lonely venture, but I was blessed from the very beginning with the support and contribution of many people who made the creation of this book a heartwarming experience. The wonderfully enthusiastic support and sensitivity of my editor, Marnie Cochran of Perseus Publishing, provided a loving home for this book. My agent, Mary Tahan of Clausen, Mays, and Tahan Literary Agency, never wavered in her belief in me and in my work and offered priceless input and guidance. I'm indebted to all the people who shared their personal stories with me, some anonymously, others using their real names, so that others could learn from their courage and find the strength within themselves to be transformed by adversity. Rabbi Moshe Dahan introduced me to the teachings of Kabbalah, which were a source of inspiration for some of the ideas expressed throughout these pages. My incredibly loving and devoted husband, Lawrence Mitnick, has kept me going through the worst of times and has made the good times even happier because he rejoices in them with me. To these people I owe a world of gratitude, not only for nourishing and sustaining me as I wrote this book but also for giving me the impetus to keep on reaching for the stars.

Introduction:
A Way to Find Meaning in Loss

This book was shaped by a tragedy that struck my younger daughter seventeen years ago when she was twenty-two. It has taken me all this time to be able to write about that terrible event and the lessons it taught me, as many people have urged me to do. I've always believed that the best books are written simply and truthfully from the heart, and I needed to give my heart ample time to heal before I could share a few powerful spiritual principles that helped me get through the tragedy and transformed my life in the process. I've seen these principles lift many others out of helplessness, depression, and despair brought on by misfortune and transform them into stronger, more loving, creative, and fulfilled people. That's why I know these principles can give anyone dealing with adversity of any kind a way to find meaning and something good in events that seem utterly meaningless and destructive.

My message is that we can all find hidden benefits in any misfortune—if we train ourselves to see adversity in a new light and respond to it creatively. We shouldn't look for "closure" or hope to go back to normal as quickly as possible. Burying the body of a loved one doesn't bring closure, nor does executing a murderer. Quickly replacing a job we've lost or a relationship that has ended isn't the answer either. The plain truth is that when tragedy or crisis strikes, no outside event will fix what has happened, and we can't "go back" to anything. Chasing after those false promises throws us off the track. We have to meet outer change with a fundamental change inside, a shift in outlook that draws upon the creativity inborn in all of us and helps us move forward to a new beginning. With this shift in outlook, we can transform fear, anger, and sadness into a new kind of inner strength that will be a lasting source of peace of mind. Then, and only then, will we find that every bad break can also be a blessing—a new sense of purpose after the death of a loved one, the discovery of undeveloped talents after the loss of a job, a refreshed appetite for living after a serious illness, becoming a more authentic person after the breakup of a relationship.

I had already finished writing the first chapter of this book and was working on the second when the worst terrorist attacks in this nation's history destroyed the World Trade Center and part of the Pentagon, killing close to three thousand people. Like every other American and most other people throughout the world, I watched the images of the imploding buildings in New York City in horror, shock, and disbelief. I wept when I saw people in flames jumping out of windows to their deaths and people on Ground Zero screaming in pain and terror as they tried to flee.

But then different images of heroism, strength, caring, generosity, and unity among Americans of all kinds began to appear everywhere we looked. We saw brave police officers, firefighters, and rescue workers putting in twenty-hour shifts, risking their lives, many dying, to try to pull people they didn't even know from the rubble. We saw people standing in line for five hours to give blood to the American Red Cross—more than 250,000 pints in that first week. We saw doctors volunteering their time around the clock to tend to the wounded while workers from nearby offices brought chairs to use as stretchers and venetian blinds for splints. We heard about fund-raising drives all across the country that brought in astonishing amounts of money, some of it coming from the piggy banks of little children. And we applauded the heroism of three passengers on the hijacked United Airlines Flight 93 who joined together to fight the terrorists, causing the plane to crash in a field near Pittsburgh instead of into the White House or the Capitol, thereby saving hundreds of lives at the expense of their own. If ever we needed proof that the worst brings out the best in people, inspiring us to new heights of courage and compassion, and that there is always a saving power within us to help us endure and grow stronger from tragedy, this series of events was it.

This book is for people dealing with any kind of misfortune, great or small, not only for those who have lost loved ones to terrorism. Whatever you experience as a painful event is a misfortune for you, regardless of how someone else might react to it. But there are important lessons about turning bad breaks into blessings that we can all learn from such a monumental tragedy as the terrorist attacks. As the shock wore off a bit and people began to contemplate the meaning of the tragedy, many saw this horrible event as an opportunity to prevent further attacks by addressing the root cause—the hatred of people who thought our nation's use of power in other parts of the world ignored their poverty and oppression. This was a chance for us to put an end to terrorism and create a global safety net, not militarily but with the kind of economic and political development that would result in a worldwide community in which we could all live in harmony. I was particularly encouraged to hear young people interpret this tragedy as a chance to help others enjoy the fruits of modernization, a chance for their

generation to change the world "for real." On a personal
level, victims' families and everyone else who felt their pain
thought the hidden good in this evil was that it made loving
the important people in our lives our highest priority.

I know that if you're grieving the devastating loss of a
loved one, I may sound like a Pollyanna who's trying to talk
you out of your suffering, but that's the last thing I want to
do. You need to experience your suffering and talk about it
with others, not repress or deny it. Otherwise your feelings
of anger, helplessness, and fear will fester quietly until they
crop up later in a more destructive way. Experience your
suffering, yes, but don't get stuck in it. If you lost someone
in the terrorist attacks, the title of this book, *What Doesn't
Kill You Makes You Stronger,* may make you think, yes, I'm
alive, but I should have been killed, not my son, my daughter, my wife, my husband, my brother firefighters, my fellow
police officers. You may feel so guilty and bereft that you
don't even want to go on. Here I am, telling you that you
can turn bad breaks into blessings, and you may be asking,
How can I possibly make any good come out of such horrible evil? Who would want to live in a world where such
soulless evil can happen?

These are all normal feelings that arise when your faith
has been shaken to the core, but if you allow anger and despair to destroy your faith and ruin your life, *you've become
your own worst enemy,* not the terrorists. The same is true
for any outside cause of your suffering. You can't always prevent disasters from happening or avoid getting hurt by them,
but how you react to them is your own choice. Disasters
can't obliterate your reason for living unless you let them.
Your pain is within your control. You can moderate the extent of your suffering by choosing to respond to any painful
situation with faith in yourself and in the mysterious work-

ings of the unseen world. If you react with despair, then you are the agent of the destruction of your own peace of mind. Internal work has to be done, and help is always available from other people and from the universe itself.

For some of you, faith is synonymous with a belief in God, however you understand God to be. But let me make it clear that you need not believe in a God concept at all to benefit from the principles you'll find in this book. Mine is not a religious approach to resilience; it's a spiritual one, showing you how to connect with a power within yourself greater than your ordinary self-awareness. You can be an atheist or an agnostic and still be able to turn bad breaks into blessings with these principles and the strategies for implementing them.

Whenever you see words such as *God, the universe, higher power,* or *the metaphysical/spiritual world* in these pages, feel free to substitute any word or words you choose that connote for you a life force or a universal free-flowing creative energy. I've never believed in the concept of God as a giant king with a white, flowing beard, seated on a throne, dishing out punishments and rewards. I think of God as the source of the pure, positive, infinite creative energy of the universe—the original and ultimate life force responsible for creating and sustaining us and directing our spiritual growth. Evil is not part of the equation, not something that is visited upon us from above. Human beings have free will; we can either succumb to our destructive impulses or resist them. The creative life force that I believe in doesn't interfere in human events and can't stop those of us who are corrupted by hatred from making evil choices. What that life force can do, if we plug in to it, is activate the spark within each of us of that radiant energy—loving, purposeful, and devoid of negativity. By staying connected to that power on an ongoing basis, we can persevere and overcome whatever misfortune strikes us and eventually find joy again.

In a sense, the war against terrorism is actually a spiritual war. We're pitted against enemies whose faith in their God gives them the courage to give up their own lives willingly, as a guaranteed entrance to heaven, in their evil mission to destroy our people and our way of life. We need to counter their faith with our own supreme faith in a God as a loving life force and not rely solely on military might or technological advances to bring us victory. What we hate in the terrorists is what we need to work on in ourselves—intolerance of anyone who is different. If the terrorist attacks on our own soil awaken us to become more actively caring toward people of difference everywhere, that will have been a major benefit of the tragedy.

I have to admit that before my personal experience with tragedy, I was never a very religious or deeply spiritual person. In fact, for all my outward bravado, I was a driven, anxious, depression-prone person who made a career of giving sage advice to others but had a hard time following it myself. My desire to help others was sincere and emotionally rewarding, but I couldn't help feeling like a failure no matter what I achieved. In fact, even before my daughter's accident—you'll find out more about that in the pages ahead—I was in such torment from striving so hard to succeed that I sought relief in one system after another. I studied psychology, Judaism, Christianity, Buddhism, New Age philosophies, the ancient Jewish mysticism known as Kabbalah, whatever I could find.

Nothing I had ever studied prepared me for a calamity of the magnitude of my daughter's accident, probably because I had never really internalized or seriously practiced the systems I'd studied. Without consciously knowing what I was doing or how I was doing it, I connected with a power greater than myself that helped pull me through this crisis and answer the inner demons that had dogged me all of my life. The reason I'd felt like a failure, I realized, was that I was looking for fulfillment in the wrong places instead of where it was all along—right under my nose. I learned that there is no deeper satisfaction in life than loving the people close to you and appreciating the gift of life itself.

It took me a long time to formulate exactly what the principles were that helped me find the hidden blessings in something I would have given my life not to have happen. Amazingly, when I did formulate a few basic principles for dealing with life's challenges, I realized that whenever I had unconsciously followed them before my daughter's accident, things turned out much better than I ever could have imagined. And when I didn't follow them, because my selfishness and desperate need for recognition took over, things didn't turn out too well. Now I understand the value of following these principles *consciously*, and teaching others how to do that as well.

I guess these principles are an amalgam of insights that came to me from the many different systems I studied, but they never really clicked in until I was put to the severest test. That was the catalyst that opened my eyes to the spiritual world beyond the five senses and made it a reality for me. I don't have scientific evidence or theological arguments or clinical studies to back up my knowledge of an unseen spiritual world and the way it influences the course of our lives in this physical world, nor do I think they're necessary. All I know is that this philosophy works. I've seen it work with countless people who were devastated by the death of a loved one or the breakup of a marriage or the loss of a job or financial ruin or serious illness or some other unexpected calamity and were able to turn their lives around. I'm a very pragmatic person, and I believe in the old saying, the proof of the pudding is in the eating. What works works; everything else is irrelevant.

The ideas in this book certainly aren't original with me, but I came to them from the inside out. For me, they had the quality of personal discovery, emanating as they did from my own experience. An influential pioneer on the subject of adapting to traumatic change is William Bridges, author of the 1980 book *Transitions* as well as *The Way of Transition*, published in 2000. His work was a springboard for some of my ideas on the process of letting go of the past after an adversity has ripped apart the structure of your life.

I firmly believe that life doesn't give us anything we can't handle—that is, if we have the right outlook and don't attempt to do it alone. If we say we can't handle it, that's a judgment call, and an unfair one, at that. Don't sell yourself short. You have it in you—we all have it in us—to find a way out of the darkness and into the light again. Creativity has been born in all of us so that the human race can adapt to change and grow from it and not sink into stagnation and chaos. Adapting to change is only half the battle; the other half is the growth part, and that takes some doing. What I'm teaching in this book is not simply resilience, but "creative resilience"—ways to negotiate the stages of the resilience journey from the darkest days to actual regeneration.

When I first began pulling my ideas together for this book, I made the mistake of talking about them with someone who just didn't get it. She said, "Oh, some people have the strength to overcome obstacles, and other people don't. You can't teach that kind of thing." What an arrogant point of view! That's like saying some people are born smart and others aren't, and the ones who aren't can never learn anything. Haven't we all heard of supposedly "dumb" students who blossomed under the tutelage of a teacher who cared about them and related to them with understanding and love? Resilience *can* be taught. It's taught everyday by ministers, therapists, and courageous role models. Some people may be more naturally resilient than others, but anyone who is willing to learn how to find blessings in adversity *will* find them.

One of the big benefits of a major crisis is that it forces you to define for yourself what's important in life, as it did for me. Most of us lead lives not of quiet desperation but of frantic distraction. We're so busy scurrying about with our personal agendas that until a wave sneaks up on us from behind and knocks us down—a tragedy such as the terrorist strikes, an illness, a divorce, a lost job, a disabling accident—we don't stop to question whether our scurrying about is all that important. That's one good that came out of the evil of September 11: In the moments before the planes crashed, the poignant phone calls from passengers saying, "I love you" to their family members made us all more aware of how precious our families are. We realized we can't assume that the people we love will be here tomorrow and how important it is to draw closer to them, telling and showing them how much we love them every day. There's nothing like a crisis to get us to reexamine our priorities and figure out how we want to live our lives and become the people we really want to be.

As reluctant as we are to ponder the meaning of life under ordinary circumstances, we're even more reluctant to think about the meaning of death. With death there's this huge fear factor that makes us want to ignore it completely until it hits close to home—we lose or almost lose someone we love, we're diagnosed with a serious illness, or we witness a tragedy like the terrorist attacks. Suddenly we find we can't avoid the subject any longer, and we start asking questions about it. Is death the absolute end or only an illusion—the death of the physical body but a return of the soul to the source of all creation? Like all spiritual questions, this one can only be answered with faith, not concrete proof in a laboratory. As yet, no one has proven conclusively that life after death is real, but no one has proven conclusively that it *isn't* real either. It all boils down to this decision: Do you want to commit yourself to a belief that gives you peace of mind even though it can't be proven, or do you want to remain skeptical and live a life hounded by fear?

Whether you believe in an afterlife, reincarnation, or nothingness after death, it's immensely comforting to know that long after you've left this earth, you can survive in the hearts of the people you have loved or contributed to in some way. Our future after death is the legacy we leave behind. Death is not nearly as frightening to me as it used to be, because I've learned that each of us has the power to create a legacy that will live on and enrich the lives of others long after we die. I've seen people who felt bereft and helpless because they knew that there was nothing they or anyone else could do that would bring a lost loved one back to life. But when they stopped thinking about the finality of physical death and started thinking about how they could make their loved ones present in their lives and honor their memories, they found comfort and a sense of purpose. They understood what immortality really is.

If you focus on giving the most of yourself while you are on this earth, then you can accept death with grace and equanimity and enjoy the richness and fullness of this life down to the very end. A lovely, gracious woman who had devoted her life to her family before losing her battle with cancer is an example. At her funeral, the rabbi told how he went to visit her on her deathbed to comfort her, and she told him something he'd never heard from anyone in those straits before. Thinking of all the people—her children, their husbands and wives, her grandchildren, her other relatives and friends— who had showered her with love as they came to say goodbye, she said, "I've had a beautiful life, and even this is beautiful."

This is a book for survivors. It's for anyone who feels frightened, sad, angry, or helpless in the face of any kind of adversity, whether it's man-made, caused by some law of nature going awry, or the result of just plain bad luck. If you're someone who is facing a misfortune we all hope we'll never have to face—the death of a loved one, the loss of a job, the breakup of a relationship, serious illness, financial ruin—the principles and strategies in this book can make your life meaningful and productive in spite of your adversity. Even though you don't think it's possible now, you'll emerge from your adversity a much stronger person psychologically, emotionally, physically, and spiritually. You'll have the confidence that you can handle just about anything. You will also posess a system of beliefs that will make you a more loving and caring person, instead of a bitter and cynical one, and bring creativity and fulfillment into your life.

In one of life's strange coincidences, this book was coming to publication when a personal crisis happened that I never would have been able to handle as well without my system of beliefs. On March 26, 2002, I was operated on for a growth in my colon that I had initially been told was benign but turned out to be malignant. Fortunately, no nodes were involved, and I was diagnosed with Stage II colon cancer. Had this happened to me in the days before I developed the outlook and strategies described in this book, my fear, anxiety, and other negative emotions probably would have had a deleterious effect on my recovery. Instead, I went home from the hospital two and a half days after abdominal surgery that usually requires a hospital stay of five days to a week. My surgeon called me a "miracle woman" and kept telling me that I had no idea how rare my quick and relatively painless recovery was. I attribute my experience in large measure to his outstanding skill as a surgeon, but I also think my principles for dealing with misfortune gave me the strength to be resilient and will continue to see me through the days ahead.

In this book I've laid out a path that takes you through four stages of recovery from an event that has torn your world apart: *rupture, reflection, rebuilding,* and *regeneration.* These aren't stages that you *have* to go through intentionally; they're simply naturally unfolding sequences of the recovery process that I've identified. There's no formula for going through them other than doing it in your own way and at your own pace, but I've given you steps to follow that will help carry you through one stage to the next.

You'll find many real-life stories in this book showing how the crises that derail us can awaken the tremendous power and potential we all have within us—our God-given creativity—and help us discover new meaning and purpose in our lives. I've tried to make these people real to you, almost like role models in a way, by giving you the details of what they did and how they did it. Follow their example, and you, too, will find the gifts in your misfortune—new insights, a greater capacity to give and receive love, more abundance, happiness based on your deepest desires and values, a new dream.

Always remember, the worst things that happen to us have the most potential to make us great. I offer you this book with love and the fervent hope that it will help you realize that potential.

Part I

Rupture

1

The Answer to "Why Me?"
—The Three Principles

This is a true story. A man who was down on his luck, out of work, and feeling hopeless about the future decided that he was going to commit suicide. He wanted to give God one last chance, so he made a deal. "God, if you want me to go on living, give me a call," he said. "I'll wait ten minutes, and if the phone doesn't ring, I'm out of here." He sat by the telephone and waited. The minutes ticked by. One . . . two . . . three . . . four . . . five . . . At the count of nine, the phone rang. The man picked it up. There was no one on the other end of the line. The man took this as a sign from God that he should not give up. He threw the pills he was going to take down the sink, got on with his life, and eventually found success.

Did God really make the phone ring, or was it pure coincidence? We'll never know. The point is, had this man given in to his darkest impulses, he never would have lived long enough to find out that the seemingly hopeless situation he was in was not hopeless at all. Help from the universe is always available to us, even in our bleakest moments, if we open our hearts to it. The moment we stand outside our-

selves and connect with a higher intelligence than our limited rational minds, we set miracles in motion.

I'm not a psychic. I don't have a crystal ball, but I can
tell you with absolute certainty that whatever excruciating
crisis you're going through right now—your spouse has left
you, you've been fired from your job, you've been diagnosed
with a serious illness—is not without hope; it has hidden
riches in it. What you wish had never happened to you will
in time bring you benefits beyond anything you can imagine
if you remove the blocks to receiving them. I know this because I've seen this phenomenon happen time and time
again in my own life and in the lives of countless people
who've come through the doors of my counseling agency
over the course of twenty-eight years. Even the premature
death of someone you love, heartbreaking as it is, can transform you and inspire you to honor that person's memory beyond anything you might have done had your loved one not
been snatched away so quickly. Some of the people you'll
meet later in this book will show you how.

The trouble with a blessing in disguise is that, because it's
hidden, it seems like nothing more than a cruel or senseless
event. When my younger daughter Rona was a teenager, she
broke her femur in a car accident. I rushed to the hospital to
find her lying on a gurney, bloodied and in pain, screaming,
"Why me?" I had no answer. All I could do was hold her
hand and try to assure her that the doctor would take care of
her, that everything would be all right—and it was.

I now know that this universal "Why me?" when misfortune strikes is not really a question but a cry of shock and
outrage at the unfairness of life. Philosophically, we might
understand that good and evil, life and death, and health
and sickness are part of the complementary positive-nega-
tive design of our physical world, that one can't exist with-

out its opposite any more than we can have light without darkness. It's only when the dark side of the moon looks down on *us* that we feel singled out for undeserved punishment. But life is just being life. Like

"Shouldn't happen what can."

my husband's Uncle Phil used to say in his untutored, immigrant wisdom, "Shouldn't happen what can."

The amazing thing is that when you ask, "Why me?" not out of paranoia but as a questioning of what your life means and how you should live it—not questioning God but questioning yourself—you immediately begin the process of transforming yourself from a hostage to fortune to the architect of your own destiny. The desire to learn, change, and grow stronger from a painful event instantly connects you to a positive energy system that not only helps you weather this storm but also gives you control over the course of your life. Staying connected to that positive energy system by following some basic principles frees you from being at the mercy of outside events and gives you a consistent feeling of inner calm and confidence. You will know that whatever is happening right now, or will happen in the future, is right for you in terms of your ultimate happiness and fulfillment.

What follows are the three principles for turning bad breaks into blessings:

1. Embrace Misfortune as an Opportunity for Transformation

Here's the number-one paradox of life: The crises that trouble us the most are the very instruments for gaining *perma-*

nent peace of mind. Your heart may be broken, but your soul must embrace these crises. The one right answer to the question, "Why me?" is to say yes to misfortune as an opportunity for transformation. Use it as a catalyst for growth. Answer the call of your soul to replace fear with certainty, being reactive with being creative, self-involvement with sharing, and you will draw positive energy that will enrich you immeasurably. Hindsight shows us that without this tragedy or trouble, such a feared and despised intruder in our lives, we might never have learned to appreciate the people who matter most to us or developed talents we didn't know we had or resolved some emotional issue or discovered how to satisfy our basic desires in some larger purpose that brings true happiness.

The answer to "Why me?" is *yes*. Embrace misfortune as an opportunity for transformation.

Surrendering to misfortune is an act of pure faith—it's knowing that in the way the spiritual world operates, an apparently bad situation is also essentially for the good in the long run. This certainty that *everything* in our physical world derives from the positive energy of the unseen spiritual world is the magic wand that transmutes the "bad things" into good. Remember those fire drills you used to have in school? The alarm scared you out of your wits until you realized that this was only a test. Well, that's how it is with our afflictions. They're not curses; they're only tests to discover whether you'll react in panic or take control of the situation for your own benefit. The real danger is the urge to abandon your faith in the creative life force of the universe and not maintain your trust in its goodness. Your conviction that something better lies ahead is the seed of its creation. What makes positive outcomes happen is not "seeing is believing"—the distrustful attitude of skeptics—but the absolute certainty that, to quote Kabbalist Rav Berg, "believing is seeing."

I realize that if you lost a loved one in the appalling terrorist attacks or your spouse has just

Believing is seeing.

—Rav Berg

died of a sudden heart attack or you've been told that the tumor you thought was benign is cancer or you learn that the healthy baby you were having has been born with defects or you've lost all your savings in an investment you hoped would make you a millionaire, you don't want to hear or can't believe that everything bad that happens can also be for the best. But the sooner you suspend your disbelief, the more quickly you will rebound. The blessing may not be visible for a long time—not until you have the 20–20 vision of hindsight—but if you believe it, you *will* see it somewhere down the line.

Adversity is like a mystery novel. The uncertainty about the outcome makes you want to jump ahead to the last page to find out how the story ends, but that would defeat the purpose of the reading experience. You can't find the rewards this crisis will bring you until you've put all the clues together and deciphered the meaning you'll ultimately attach to it. You'll know how you've come out ahead after you've gone the full distance—gone through your sadness, fear, anger, confusion, and the whole process of rebuilding your life and establishing new connections. Then you'll find that this crisis has remade you into a wiser, deeper, even happier person than you were before. If you knew in advance why this misfortune could be the best thing that ever happened to you, you'd miss the whole point of the exercise.

You would not keep looking for the pony in the pile of manure until you find it.

Only in retrospect, when you look back on painful, tragic events that tear your world apart, can you see that there is always unexpected good buried somewhere in the worst. For now, you have to believe that, believe it with all your heart. Holding fast to that belief when you think that life has treated you badly will give you the power to persevere until the answer to the question, "Why me?" becomes manifest.

2. The Inner Shift: Reframe Loss as Possibility

Let me tell you briefly about four people who emerged from the adversities that befell them stronger, wiser, and more fulfilled after undergoing the first crucial step on the journey toward transformation—an inner shift in outlook. Instead of focusing on the pain of loss, they redirected their thoughts to the promise of possibility.

Joanne

Joanne was diagnosed with stomach cancer only three years after her husband had been killed in a freak boating accident, leaving her the single mom of two young children. At first she was overwhelmed by grief and fear at this threat to her life so soon after losing her husband. "I was starting to feel cursed," she says. "I had no idea how I was going to be able to work, take care of my kids, and be a cancer victim all at the same time."

Joanne was sitting in her doctor's office, leafing through pamphlets about her illness when she came across a sentence that blew her mind: *A cancer survivor is anyone with a diagnosis of cancer.* "A lightbulb went off in my head," Joanne says. "Suddenly I had a whole new perspective on my illness! I wasn't a victim of cancer any more; now I saw myself as a survivor." With that change in attitude, Joanne began to take charge of her health and the direction of her life. "I couldn't control what had happened to my body," she says, "but I could control my reactions, my state of mind."

For Joanne, having a life-threatening disease made her more keenly aware and appreciative of all small things that gave her joy in life—smiles and hugs from her kids, walking in the park, chatting with her friends. Her illness also made her rethink how she wanted to spend the rest of her life. She quit her job in advertising and went to work for a public health organization, disseminating information that could save people's lives. After long months of chemotherapy, and six

Reframe loss as possibility. See yourself not as a victim but as a survivor.

years after her diagnosis, Joanne is healthy again. "My cancer was a gift," she says. "I feel more alive than I ever did before. I'm not just living life now; I'm loving it. I'm thankful for every day I wake up."

Terry

Terry was one of more than a thousand people who lost their jobs when the plant where he was a manager closed. At forty-five, having worked for the same company all his adult life, Terry was scared to strike out on his own, but something deep inside him gave him the courage. "I asked myself, what do I want to be doing with my life five years from now, ten years from now?" he remembers. "Was being a plant manager all I was cut out to be?"

After doing a lot of soul-searching, Terry decided that he wasn't really a company man. "All along I had a low-level feeling of frustration at not being my own boss," he says. "It never occurred to me that I *could* be my own boss, but getting laid off was a wake-up call. 'This isn't a bad break,' I thought to myself, 'it's your chance. Take it. You know what you lost; let's see what you can find.'" Terry used his severance pay to open a bike repair shop out of his garage. Business has been phenomenal. "I'll be financially secure for the rest of my life," Terry says gratefully. "Losing my job brought me what I always wanted. I'm living out my boyhood dream of owning my own business and doing work I love instead of just holding down a job."

Kay

Kay was in her midthirties, a mother whose life revolved around her three young children, when her husband Barry came home with the news that he was leaving her for a woman he'd fallen in love with at work. "It was like the sun, the moon, and the stars had fallen down on me," Kay says. "I did nothing but walk around in my bathrobe and cry for days on end. I felt like a complete failure as a woman." She was furious at Barry, not only for his infidelity but also for forcing her into the job market out of financial necessity. "I resented having to go back to work before I was ready," Kay recalls, "but underneath my resentment was this giant glob of fear."

On reflection, Kay realized that motherhood had consumed her so much that she'd shut Barry out and stopped growing in many ways. Suddenly, she saw having to go back to work in a new light. "Instead of resenting it, I saw it as a chance to stop hiding out from the world under the cover of being a great mom," Kay says, "and do something about becoming a great person." Kay decided to channel her love of children into a profession. Still a "great mom," she now has a master's degree in education and was recently named teacher of the year at her school. She has also found love again. Her new husband says, "I thought I'd never fall in love again after my wife died of breast cancer, but then Kay came along—her warmth, sparkle, and compassion are amazing."

Howard

You may remember Howard Lutnick. On September 11, 2001, Lutnick, CEO of Cantor Fitzgerald, a bond trading firm, lost more than 600 of the 1,000 men and women who worked in the firm's New York offices in the World Trade Center. One of the victims was Lutnick's own thirty-six-year-old brother, Gary. Lutnick was spared only because he had taken his five-year-old son to his first day of grade school that morning and arrived at the World Trade Center just in time to flee for his life. The tragedy scorched Lutnick's heart. Despite his reputation for being ruthless in business, he couldn't stop crying openly in public, at times saying helplessly, "I can't stand it."

But unbelievably, only two days later Lutnick and some surviving employees reopened the company's electronic bond trading network in a backup office and were conducting business. What galvanized this incredible comeback? It was the strong conviction on the part of Lutnick and his staff that the firm had to survive and prosper to take care of the bereaved families who were suddenly dependent on it—the firm's "new class of partners," as Lutnick told the *New York Times*. Lutnick went to work immediately to help these people, setting up a family service center in a Manhattan hotel, giving out his home phone number to every one of them and encouraging them to call, and negotiating with an insurance company to get them generous benefits. Lutnick also set up the Cantor Fitzgerald Foundation to aid the families of all World Trade Center victims, no matter where they worked, and donated $1 million of his own money to it. In an interview on *Good Morning America*, Lutnick said his hard-nosed view of business had changed, and he had found a new sense of purpose: "We've got to make our company able to take care of our families." Once criticized for being too aggressive, Lutnick emerged from the tragedy as one of our nation's most admired and compassionate business leaders.

For all four of these people, the defining moment came when they looked out on that terrifying blank space between the past reality they had known and the new reality yet to come, and instead of seeing nothing, they saw possibility. Joanne saw the possibility of being a survivor; Terry saw the possibility of starting his own business; Kay saw the possibility of personal growth; Howard Lutnick saw the possibility of restarting his company to take care of the victims' families. These people redefined or reframed their particular crisis as a chance. They gained control over the situation by shifting their focus from what had been lost to new avenues they could explore. As Joanne said, she couldn't control the changes that affected her physically, but she could control how she perceived and reacted to them. That's all any of us can control. Assuming control of our outlook is the first step in rebounding from a crisis and ultimately being transformed by it.

It's been said that luck is what happens when preparation meets opportunity. That's very true, but first you have to recognize an opportunity when it comes knocking—and that's not easy to do when it blows your whole house down. There you are, sitting in the rubble of your family structure or your broken-down body or your bombed-out work life, and you can't see past the tears in your eyes. Grieving fully and openly for what has been lost is a necessary part of recovery. You have to do it at your own pace, but looking at your situation from the angle of possibility rather than loss will make the pain more bearable and the suffering less prolonged. Your depression will start to lift when, instead of seeing nothingness ahead, you see images of things you can do—go back to school, search for information on the Internet, join an organization, volunteer for a charity, pursue a lifelong dream. It's like looking at two faces peering at each other in a Rorschach test and refocusing your eyes so that you suddenly see a goblet in the dark space between them.

Transformation begins when you meet outer changes with an internal shift in outlook and you reframe loss as possibility. Change your outlook, and you change your luck. Shift from a victim to a survivor mentality, and you can go on to create a new reality for yourself that surpasses the old.

Here are a few examples of how a victim reacts and a survivor prevails:

- A victim asks how long will it take to feel good—a survivor decides to feel good even if things are not so great.
- A victim grinds to a halt—a survivor keeps putting one foot in front of the other.
- A victim wallows in self-pity—a survivor comforts others.

- A victim is jealous of someone else's success—
  a survivor is inspired by it.
- A victim focuses on the pain of loss—a survivor cherishes remembered joy.
- A victim seeks retribution—a survivor seeks
  redemption.
- And most of all, a victim argues with life—a
  survivor embraces it.

3. Let Go of Who You Were and Become More of Who You Are

A Mother's Story

The telephone call came early on a Sunday morning in June. My husband was downstairs, getting ready to go out jogging, and I was still lazily luxuriating in bed. I picked up the phone groggily, and I could not believe what I was hearing. It was my ex-husband calling to tell me that our daughter Rona, the same one who'd been injured in an automobile accident six years earlier, had again been in a car accident, this one involving a drunken driver. She was in a coma in Baylor Hospital in Dallas, brain-injured and fighting for her life. I heard myself screaming, "No! No! No!" It was so incomprehensible. *Brain-injured?* Not Rona. She was a talented journalist who'd been a star as managing editor of her college newspaper four years in a row at Northwestern University's prestigious Medill School of Journalism, and already, at only twenty-two, was the award-winning news editor of a daily paper in Arlington, Texas. Everyone predicted a Pulitzer in her future. How could this have happened to my baby, a gifted, sweet-natured, delicate beauty who had never hurt a living creature in her life? Why Rona? Why her?

I hung up the phone in a daze. Without really knowing what I was doing, I threw some things together in an overnight bag (I had no idea how long I'd be staying) and booked two airplane flights to Dallas. My husband, Larry, and I had been married only two years, and he hardly knew Rona since she'd been away at school most of the time that we were courting, but he wouldn't let me make that trip alone.

As soon as we were airborne, my shock gave way to feelings of guilt that were heavier and more impenetrable than the clouds outside my window. I was overwhelmed by remorse for not being a good mother to Rona in her growing-up years, for being too busy to pay attention to her when I should have because I was so driven to succeed as a writer, the head of a counseling agency, and a radio talk show host. All the ways that I had ignored her punctured my heart like a pack of knives. I thought of the mornings I'd been too tired to get out of bed and send her off to school with a kiss after I'd been up all night writing and the nights I wasn't home to cook a meal because I was working late at the office or hanging out at the station. I remembered the time she came home from summer camp and I was so involved with one of my projects that I forgot to pick her up. She and her sister had been gone two whole months, and after the bus dropped them off, they were left standing in the empty parking lot like two forlorn orphans until someone called and I came and got them. The look on her face of disappointment and forbearance came back to haunt me. How could I have been so neglectful? Where were my priorities? I cursed my ambition for being a thief and stealing so many precious moments that Rona and I could have had together. If only I had it to do over again, I would have been there for her when I wasn't there. The tears would not stop coming.

What tortured me the most was that it was *my* car Rona was in when the accident happened. I'd lent it to her because the old wreck she'd been driving had finally fallen apart. To save her money, I told her she could use my car for a while, and I would lease another one for myself. I thought she'd be safe because the car I lent her had seat belts that wrapped around you automatically as soon as you got in. How was I to know that she would find the seat belts too confining and dismantle them? Still, I blamed myself for handing her the instrument of her destruction, like a mother who feeds her child mushrooms that turn out to be poisonous. The road to hell, I kept telling myself, is paved with good intentions.

When I got to the hospital, the sight of Rona hooked up to a ventilator, tubes running in and out of her body, brought me to my knees. I was overcome by waves of pity and terror. All I wanted to do was leap into the bed and take her place—free her to get up and walk away and be the way she was when she was born. The enormity of the loss, barely sinking in, was unthinkable. I grasped her hand, cold and unresponsive, and began talking to her in a wild rush of words. "Rona, I love you so much. I'm so sorry. Don't be afraid. Can you hear me? Hang on. I know you can make it. Please don't leave me. *Please.*"

I don't know how long I stayed there, but when I got up, I moved like a robot, out of my body, observing what was happening as if it were a movie. I could hear people talking to me, and hear myself answering, but everything around me was enveloped in a cottony fog, blurred and indistinct. The young man who'd been driving the car, a photographer friend of Rona's at the newspaper, approached me in blood-spattered clothes, beside himself with grief for what he had done. He'd gone out with Rona for a couple of beers after work and didn't realize he'd had too much to drink when he got behind the wheel to drive back to the office where his motorcycle was parked. I should have been happy for him that he'd been wearing his seatbelt and got only a scratch on his nose, but I felt enraged.

On autopilot, I walked to a telephone in the hall and called my insurance agent to make sure that the accident was covered, dimly aware on some level that Rona would need an enormous amount of money. When I hung up, a man was standing there. He enveloped me in his arms and pressed his tear-stained cheek against mine, murmuring that he was sorry. It occurred to me that he was the father of the driver of the car.

The neurosurgeon, a tall, gray-haired, benevolent man, hugged me next. Wanting to prepare me for the worst, he told me that Rona had only a 10 percent chance of survival. I was stunned. I went back to the guest suite in the hospital where my husband and I would be staying indefinitely and threw myself face down on the bed. That's when I gave up any illusion of control over the situation and surrendered it all to God. I saw myself standing on the brink of a high hill, peering out into the black hole of death, and prayed that the razor-thin line of connection between Rona and me in this life would not break.

The next days and weeks were an exercise in the agony of uncertainty. Every four hours they let me into the ICU, and I watched Rona, minute by minute, struggling to breathe with every fiber of her being, a study in the will to survive. I cried, "Stop!" to myself every time the thought that she might not make it entered my mind, and I banished the thought of her in a permanent vegetative state the same way. Once, when all the bells and whistles of the machinery she was hooked up to went off, I ran out of the room in alarm, yelling for the nurse, who came in and told me that nothing was wrong—Rona had coughed. Another time, when I'd reached a point where I was terrified of going into her room and finding the bed empty, I sent my husband in instead. I waited in the hall, staring through the plate-glass window in the door, and when Larry gave me the thumbs-up sign, I mustered the strength to go through that door yet another time.

If it hadn't been for Larry, I don't know how I would have gotten through the two months I spent in Dallas. Even though he had business to do at home, he never left my side. He supported and nurtured me, and at night when we were lying in bed, he held me and let me cry my heart out, which was something I needed to do. The murderous rage I felt toward the driver of the car and at the unfairness of life—my daughter nearly dead and the driver with a scratch on his nose—made me rant like a lunatic about revenge fantasies at times. I'm sure they frightened Larry, but he didn't show it. He simply answered me with calm logic until I became rational again. We were virtually still on our honeymoon, and when I apologized to him for not being able to make love, he said, thinking of Rona lying elsewhere in the hospital, barely clinging to life, "That would be a sacrilege."

Larry also understood the importance of taking care of yourself in little ways when you're in crisis and insisted that we go out for dinner some nights at the finer restaurants in town. Those outings refreshed me, but I was so depressed that I could hardly eat at all—this woman, who had always battled a weight problem, who was constantly dieting and craving a sinful chocolate dessert, couldn't get a morsel down.

My family and friends kept calling from home, and my older daughter, Ilene, came from law school to be at her sister's bedside with me. Just having them listen quietly to me as I put my feelings into words was like a safety valve that kept me from exploding when I felt overwhelmed by grief, rage, anxiety, or despair. The outpouring of cards, letters, and gifts from listeners to my radio show, after word got back to them, helped to keep me afloat, too. They shared stories of similar tragedies, and I thought, "If they can do it, so can I." Never underestimate the uplifting power of connection when you feel leveled by circumstances beyond your control.

The people I sat with in the ICU waiting room every day were another impromptu support group. We were like survivors of a shipwreck who'd been thrown together in a life raft. Two sisters were there because their mother had been stricken with a heart attack. A Hispanic couple had a five-year-old son on life support after he'd been hit by a truck and thrown off his bike. A feisty retired nurse, whose sister was dying from a bowel obstruction, reminisced about their childhood in the South, climbing trees with her sister and pelting people below them with chinaberries from homemade slingshots. Another woman, divorced, whose ex-husband never showed up, was bearing up remarkably well after their two sons had *both* been paralyzed on the same day, July 4, in a motorcycle accident on their way to see some fireworks. As diverse as we were, we drew comfort from each other, not because misery loves company but because empathy builds strength.

The family I remember most were the relatives of a twenty-year-old man who was waiting for a heart transplant. Tragically, it didn't come in time. I had just left Rona's room when a Code Blue team rushed past me and entered the young man's room. Through the open door I caught a glimpse of the team working frantically to save him. After a few moments, they stopped. The young man's mother emerged from the room, her head bowed in grief, another woman's arm draped around her shoulders. They walked, as if moving to a dirge, toward the handful of other relatives waiting silently for them at the end of the hall. With immense dignity in their sorrow, they all joined hands and formed a prayer circle and said their last good-byes. That image has stayed with me as a testament to the pain of loss and the beauty of connectedness that makes loss bearable—what being human is all about.

The longer Rona stayed in the ICU, the bleaker her future began to look. Each time I entered her room, my hopes were dashed with the same grim words from a tight-lipped doctor or nurse: "No change." Living in that awful limbo between fearing the worst and hoping for the best taught me a valuable lesson about uncertainty. You can only master uncertainty—a state of not knowing—by accepting that the outcome *is* unknowable, letting go of any preconceived ideas of it and having the *blind* faith that whatever the outcome is, you'll be able to handle it.

This may sound crazy, but it's even more important to let go of unduly optimistic thoughts than it is to let go of pessimistic ones. Pessimism drags your mood down and saps your energy, but with optimism, you get attached to the outcome. One night, a nurse who was with me at Rona's bedside told me about her brother, a swimming champion who'd been brain-injured diving into a pool and suffered severe impairment of his mobility. He was certain that rehabilitation would make him as good as new, and he'd go back to being an athlete again in a couple of years. When that didn't happen, he felt he'd lost everything worthwhile and couldn't see anything of value to replace it. He sat down at the kitchen table when no one was home, managed to aim a rifle at his head, and pulled the trigger.

The nurse blurted out her story unthinkingly, not meaning any harm, and while it certainly wasn't comforting, it made me realize that acceptance means letting go—letting go of the way you have always been or thought your world would always be. You don't let go of a spouse who has died (more about that later); you let go of how you were in that relationship and the belief that you would have it forever. And you don't let go of your unique and glorious soul when you lose your mobility; you let go of being able-bodied and your assumption that you would live out your life that way. You can't begin to create a new life for yourself, not simply as a survivor but as a joyful participant in the world of the living with its infinite possibilities for happiness, until you let go of the way you existed before.

Every disappointment should make you ask, "What part of the way I have always been must I let go?" Even the little everyday challenges that try your patience or provoke your anger are lessons in the need for letting go. Every time you get angry, put aside your hostility and focus on a resolution. When you lose patience, drop your insistence on being right and look at things from the other person's perspective; or conversely, lessen your need for acceptance and set better boundaries. Every unwelcome event is a call to let go of some outworn idea and learn something new, acquire some wisdom that will move your soul farther along its evolutionary path, bringing you ever closer to fulfilling your purpose in the world. Adversity is a bumpy ride, but it can be an unparalleled way to get you to your destination on this journey we call life.

> **Acceptance means letting go— letting go of the way you have always been or thought your world would always be.**

My daughter drove that lesson home to me when she came out of the coma after five weeks and began the glacially slow, incredibly frustrating process of recovery. Even without speaking, she communicated a fierce resolve to get on with her life, and I committed myself to helping her. I took a leave of absence from my job as a radio talk show host so that I could devote myself to her rehabilitation. That was the opportunity I saw in this devastation—a chance to redo those early years when I'd been obsessed with my career. Now I could expiate my deep feelings of guilt, my remorse for being an absent mother, and assist hands-on in the rebirth of my damaged child from a state of almost total helplessness to an independent life. My sense of purpose gave me little time to be depressed.

In the beginning, because she couldn't speak, I wasn't even sure Rona knew who I was. I felt terribly isolated from her, but one day, when I was bending over her while she was doing her physical exercises in rehab, I thought I heard the sound of a faint "M" emanating from her throat. I bent closer, and this time I heard several "Ms" in a row—"M . . . m . . . m." She was trying to say "Mom!" I was overjoyed. Not only did she know who I was, she would eventually speak.

After rehab I took Rona home to live with us. There was a burst of progress at first, and then came dreary plateaus where nothing seemed to happen. Her ataxia, uncontrollable tremors brought on by neurological damage, made even tying a shoelace a triumph. By dint of sheer will, she was able to compensate enough to use her computer, and little by little, some of her considerable journalistic skills began creeping back.

I always knew Rona had talent, but it wasn't until I began poring over the boxes and boxes of articles and letters she'd written, along with all the other memorabilia sent home from Texas, that I realized just how gifted she was. More than that, through this treasure trove of artifacts, the whole record of her lifetime before the accident, I came to know Rona—to see her and understand her—more than I ever had before. It was like stopping to look at a beautiful garden that you'd always passed by on your way to work and suddenly noticing the brilliant formation of colors, shapes, and textures that made it so lovely. I never could have imagined how this tragedy would bring my daughter home to me in the most profound sense.

A Daughter's Courage

After years of intensive therapy, it became clear that while Rona's intelligence and personality were still intact, she would probably never walk again unassisted or speak without a severe impairment. As devastating as her loss of motor control was, the violation of her speech was even more catastrophic. Here was a young woman whose love of language was practically her whole life. Always relentless in pursuit of a story, Rona would often pull all-nighters at school with her friends at the *Daily Northwestern*, feeding their coffee addiction and talking, talking, talking until the sun came up. For a person who was so verbally expressive as well as a talented writer, it was particularly cruel to be thrust into a world where her every attempt to say something was met with uncomprehending stares.

Even I had to struggle to understand her. She would be patient about it, good-natured at first, spelling out words by letter and using hand gestures to convey what she was saying. But then, when I still couldn't understand her, she would erupt in rage and frustration and burst into tears.

Inside I wept along with her. When we went out socially or had people come visit us, it was even more painful. After making a valiant but doomed attempt to communicate with her, everyone soon gave up. They simply had no tools for grasping what she was trying to say and would begin chatting over her head or around her as if she were invisible. My husband and I tried to engage her but couldn't. She would sit there watching silently, isolated, her nose pressed against the conversational windowpane.

Within two years, Rona was able to move out of our home and enter a community-based program. With awe-inspiring determination and courage that never quit, she began to rebuild her life as a disabled person. At first she shied away from anything that even had the word *disabled* in it, but gradually she began to let go of the life she'd had before, of speaking normally and walking independently, and see the possibilities in her changed circumstances. Always an idealist who wanted to make the world a better place as a newspaper reporter and editor, she found something that gave her a new sense of purpose—championing the cause of people with disabilities. This is not to say that she didn't grieve for her loss. Sometimes she would cry inconsolably for "what I used to do but can't do now," as she put it with poignant simplicity, but finding meaning in her misfortune kept her from getting bogged down in the swamp of self-pity.

Eight years after the accident, by the time she was thirty, Rona was able to move into her own apartment in Philadelphia and, with some help from home care aides, live independently. She got a part-time volunteer job with a suburban newspaper and began turning out eye-opening articles about how society denies disabled people their civil rights. After one of her articles made its way into the *Philadelphia Daily*

News, a local TV show invited the two of us on as guests. As I sat beside her during the interview, listening to all the people calling in gratefully to say what an inspiration she was to them, I felt proud. I saw that even strangers were awed by the way she'd seized upon this terrible thing that had happened to her as an instrument for spiritual growth, speaking out against injustice even more loudly than she had before the accident robbed her of speech. As it always does for those who will let it, adversity brought Rona a giant step closer toward being the person she was meant to be. Later, she actually said to me, "The ride of my life—or almost death—hasn't stopped me from wanting to shine light on dark corners. I'm more *me* than ever."

Another big moment came for us when Rona was declared legally competent to handle her affairs. Can you imagine what it was like for me to stand in Orphan's Court—the very name made me shudder—and ask to have her declared legally *incompetent* when she was in coma? It took a three-year-long court battle before a wonderfully humane judge, Francis X. O'Brien, restored her to full competency. After watching her make her way slowly into his chambers on a walker and listening to her testify in her own behalf, along with her lawyer, the judge wrote in his decision, "Ms. Schnall is a living example of what we mean by the word courage."

Love's Grand Design

Eventually, Rona became involved in Americans Disabled for Attendant Programs Today (ADAPT), an organization fighting to make it possible for people with disabilities to live in the community with real supports instead of being locked away in nursing homes or institutions. It was at one of

ADAPT's conventions in Nashville that love walked into Rona's life—or should I say, rolled in. She was at a table in her wheelchair having her morning coffee by herself when an attractive guy in his mid-thirties, with a thick head of black hair and a luxurious beard, wheeled over to her in his electric scooter and tried to strike up a conversation. He was friendly and outgoing, and he had a languorous Texan drawl.

"Hi, I'm David Wittie, your team leader," he said, glancing at Rona's identification badge pinned to her jacket. "How're you'all doin', Rona? Where're you from?"

Rona kept her nose buried in her newspaper, ignoring him. "I didn't think he would understand me," Rona says, "so I thought, what's the use of answering him." She couldn't face going through the same old torturous hassle, repeating and repeating herself, only to draw a blank stare and be rejected yet again.

"That must be an interesting article you're reading," David said, trying a different tack. "What's it about?" Again Rona ignored him, hoping he'd get the message and go away. But David persisted: "I can tell you're not in the best of moods this morning. Anything I can do to help?"

Now Rona was getting angry. "It annoyed me that he wouldn't back off," she says. "I felt very defensive. I didn't want to talk, and I thought he was invading my space." She decided to get rid of him rudely, mincing no words, since he—like everyone—wouldn't understand her anyway.

"Leave me alone, jerk," she said. "You're bothering me. Get lost." Abruptly, she grabbed her newspaper and started wheeling away from him when she heard David say,

"I'll leave you alone, but don't call me a jerk. I didn't mean to bother you. I just saw you sitting by yourself and wanted to know if you were okay." Rona stopped dead in her tracks. She couldn't believe it—David was responding to her *word for word.* Was this possible? She turned and looked at him incredulously.

"You understand me?"

David nodded. "Sure."

Rona's face broke into a broad smile—the smile of a traveler lost in the desert, dying of thirst, who suddenly stumbles upon water. Miraculously, she'd met the one person who could decipher what all the others, even her own mother, found incomprehensible. She'd found the one person—a complete stranger—who could give her back the precious gift of being understood.

"Now that we cleared that up," David said, grinning, "Can I buy you another cup of coffee?"

Rona came back to the table and began a conversation with David that has never ended. David told her that he grew up in a small town in Texas, lived in Austin, was a graduate of the University of Texas, and was paralyzed from the waist down from polio he contracted when he was five years old (his parents had been afraid to have him vaccinated because they'd been told that the vaccine was unsafe). They discovered that they'd both been communications majors in college and had more in common than either had imagined.

When Rona phoned home excitedly to tell me she'd met someone, I had an even harder time understanding her than when we talked in person. There was a pause, and within seconds David came on the line. He introduced himself and said, "Your daughter just said, 'I'm having a wonderful time in Nashville—better than I expected.'"

I was startled. I could feel goose bumps rising on my arms. Out of nowhere an intermediary had suddenly appeared, and through him I could do what I had despaired of being able to do. I could talk to my daughter again!

Not long after that, David came to Philadelphia to stay with Rona for a two-week visit. One afternoon while she was working at the newspaper, I took him out to lunch. He told me how he knew from the first that he wanted to spend the rest of his life with Rona. I asked him what it was about her that had drawn him to her so.

"She was so articulate," he said.

Tears welled up in my eyes. How blessed we all were, I thought, that he could find that out. He went on, "She was more interesting than anyone I'd spoken to in a long time. I was impressed with her deep commitment to making a difference."

David asked Rona to follow him to Texas later, and she accepted. I gave them my blessing. What seemed incredible to me was that almost from the time she regained consciousness, Rona had been hankering to return to Texas. She had no memory of the accident. All she could recall of Texas was that Arlington was the last place she'd been before her life was radically interrupted. With David, she'd be starting her new life almost in the same spot where the old one had ended.

Rona and David have been living together in their own apartment in Austin for seven years now, devoted to each other and to a common cause larger than themselves, traveling extensively, participating in rallies and demonstrations (even getting arrested at times), lecturing on disability rights at local colleges, fighting court battles that are changing the shape of the lives of the disabled not only in Texas but nationally. They are also enjoying a richness of life I wouldn't have thought possible—socializing with a wide circle of friends and going out to dinner, movies, and concerts like any other couple who can walk on their own two feet. That's another gift conferred by the tragedy. Nearly losing her life motivated Rona, who had always been a driven workaholic like her mother, to slow down and make more time for pleasure.

As I watched Rona's relationship with David unfold, I started pondering its mystical meaning. Their backgrounds couldn't have been more dissimilar. David was from a poor family in Texas, descended from grandparents who chopped cotton in the fields. Rona, on the other hand, was a doctor's daughter who grew up in upper-middle-class affluence in suburban Philadelphia. Yet the attraction between them was obvious. Besides both having been grievously hurt by life, they shared the same worldview and deeply held convictions, the same way with words and ironic sense of humor, and the same activist spirit. There was also the complementary yin/yang of his openness and her reserve, his organizational mind and her creativity, his teddy bearishness and her fragility.

I realized that Rona never would have met David if she hadn't been thrown through the windshield of a car on a highway in Dallas late on a summer night. I kept thinking about something a friend of hers said when the accident first happened and I kept crying out, "Why Rona? Why her?" Lisa Pope, her closest friend from college, who rushed to her side at the hospital and helped me through the worst, answered, "Who else would God scoop up and save?"

No one can say why one person is spared and another isn't or that one person deserves to live more than any other, but I knew what Lisa meant. Rona was so determined to leave an indelible mark on the world, she probably *willed* herself to stay alive. The truth is, it just wasn't her time; the rest of her story was still to be written. Even before David came into her life, she knew what her calling was. And when David connected with her so incredibly at their first meeting, it seemed like proof of love's mysterious grand design: Rona and David, both champions for social change, had been brought together to be allies on their mission in life and loving companions prevailing over their terrible deprivations with grace and courage.

The Hidden Gifts

I, too, had been transformed through Rona's accident. If it hadn't happened, I never would have come to know her in the depths of my heart as I do now. I wouldn't have become the mother to her that I became—the mother she deserved and longed for but grew up without—had she not been returned to me in a way that brought us closer than the act of birth itself. I still remember a magical bonding moment when she was living at home with us soon after the accident. I had just finished helping her bathe and was blow drying her hair, reveling in how beautiful she was, when, without a word, she turned and gave me the most incredibly loving smile. That one smile meant more to me than all the superficial glory I had been chasing after in my career. Finally, I had recovered precious and powerful feelings of maternal love long diverted into the pursuit of professional success, and I felt enormous gratitude for what I still had in spite of everything that was lost.

My whole perspective on life was also transformed by this adversity. I came away from it with more of the survivor mentality—the "this, too, shall pass" attitude—that reduced the challenges of daily living to their proper size. When Rona had progressed enough for me to return to work, I found that I could handle the stress of being a radio call-in talk show host with greater equanimity. Rude callers, flak from management, engineers who fell asleep at the switch—

nothing bothered me. Having come through a heartbreaking tragedy, I saw these everyday upsets that used to drive me up a wall for what they were: a mere blip on the screen of life. I had become a recovering drama queen. What's more, I had developed a deeper compassion for others that made me a better talk show host. No longer was I a disembodied voice coming out of my listeners' radios; I was a real human being who had been terribly hurt by life, even as many of them had been, and had grown from the ordeal.

Use my example to know that something good will come out of whatever trouble or tragedy you're facing now. It may be exactly what you've always wanted, or it may take a wholly different form, but at the end of the day you'll emerge from this crisis a stronger, wiser, more authentic person—more "me" than ever, as Rona put it. You have the same power within you that Rona and I found—the same power discovered by all the other people you'll be meeting in this book—because that power is inborn in all of us as part of our human inheritance. It's the power to create something new out of the old, the thumbprint of the original act of creation wired into every human being. Each Big Bang that disrupts our private world gives us the opportunity to create a new reality—new ways of thinking, feeling, and being—with rich rewards in all aspects of our lives: relationships, health, finances, career, family, spiritual development. To access your creative power, remember the three seminal instructions this chapter has given you:

1. Embrace misfortune as an opportunity for transformation.
2. Reframe loss as possibility.
3. Let go of the way you were, and open yourself to becoming more of who you are.

In the pages ahead, you'll learn the steps to take, along with a series of strength-building exercises, to carry out these instructions and find a meaningful answer to the question, "Why me?" Your new survivor consciousness will shield you from anxiety and depression whenever times of crisis occur, and you will learn that you can have peace of mind and continual, lasting happiness—"unconditional happiness," as I call it—independent of outside events, good or bad. Let these words from Anne Beattie's book *Perfect Recall* be your guide. Carry them in the back of your mind like a spiritual bumper sticker wherever you go: "What happens can't be stopped. Aim for grace."

Strength-Building Exercise: "This, Too, Shall Pass."

Every crisis that interrupts the smooth flow of your life makes you feel helpless and out of control. This is too much for me, you tell yourself, I can't handle this. You feel a jumble of emotions—anger, sadness, guilt, and most of all, fear—fear that you'll never love again, fear that you'll end up destitute, fear that you won't make the right decisions, fear that you'll cave in under the stress and have a breakdown, fear that you'll never find anything in life worth living for again. You forget that throughout all your life, from childhood on, you have suffered losses. At the time, they seemed insurmountable, too. Do you remember how devastated you were in grade school when your pet was run over by a car or in junior high when your best friend moved away or in high school when the college of your choice turned you down? Those losses seem small in comparison to what you're going through now, but they were larger than life then. Somehow you managed to get over them, and the loss strengthened you in some way, if only by showing you that life is full of possibilities—other pets, other friends, other schools.

Now you must learn to get control over your fears, self-doubts, and feelings of hopelessness and begin to fill the void in your life with possibilities, as you did before. One way to see beyond your present situation to a better future is, paradoxically, to look back into your past. Try to remember the worst crises you went through before this one—a broken relationship; the death of a parent, sibling, or friend; getting turned down for a job you desperately wanted; losing your most precious possessions in a burglary or a fire; having a project you worked hard on for a long time not come to fruition; getting betrayed by a friend or coworker; getting pregnant, only to have a miscarriage; losing a sizable amount of money in an investment—or anything else you can think of that crushed your spirit at the time.

I want you to reconstruct the scenario in its entirety, writing down the answers to these questions or tape recording them:

- How did you first react to the adversity? What thoughts did you have?
- What feelings did the crisis arouse in you— fear, anxiety, anger, guilt, sadness, a determination to come out ahead?
- How long did you feel immobilized, and when did you begin to recover?
- What strengths did you discover in yourself that helped you bounce back?
- Do the material things you lost still seem as important to you now?

- What did you learn from this hardship? How did overcoming it change your life?

After you've revisited these past misfortunes, please answer this one question for me: Didn't what you thought would kill you turn out to make you stronger in the long run? Haven't any of your losses made you a better person in some way, bestowed benefits you never expected? I know that was certainly true for Rona and for me as well. It was losing almost everything that taught us to value what we did have and rejoice in it. The pain will lessen in time, but don't expect it to disappear. It will be a muted pain, always there, somewhere off in the distance, and there's a reason for its existence: Joy will be even sweeter because of it. I urge you to accept your misfortune—embrace it as an opportunity to grow into a stronger, more loving, and authentic person—and you, too, will find the gift it has to offer you.

2

Connecting with the "Field of Answered Prayers"

Kaile Warren, a native of Cumberland, Maine, was in his twenties when his father died and left a small construction business for Kaile and his mother to run. Unable to afford college and become an architect, as he'd always wanted, Kaile managed to see the opportunity in adversity and eventually expanded the company from routine carpentry to new home building. He was married and had his own home, a car, and a truck when the ladder of success he was climbing came tumbling down on top of him. A serious car accident tore up his neck and shoulder and forced him out of work. The unpaid bills mounted day by day, and he ended up losing everything—his business, his home, his car, his truck, and worst of all, his wife.

Overwhelmed by so much loss, Kaile gave up on himself. His normally optimistic, go-getter outlook failed him. For two years he walked the streets of Portland, Maine, and kept spiraling downward until he wound up living in a homeless shelter, under a bridge, and in empty buildings. Then one night while he was sleeping in the abandoned warehouse that he called home, a huge rat ran across his feet. He got

up, got rid of the rat, lay back down again, and starting crying. "I prayed for intervention," Kaile says, "and this is the
strangest thing that ever happened to me in my life—the
power of this feeling that came over me. I woke up at three
o'clock that morning with this idea of a home repair business called Rent-a-Husband®, with the motto, 'Rent-a-
Husband® for those jobs that never get done.' I saw a vision
of how to market this company and how to manage it, build
it out and franchise it, and turn it into a national brand-
name service. Three weeks to the day after I came up with
the idea, I was sitting on the *Maury Povich Show,* telling my
story to a national audience. Ever since, my life and this
business have just been a whirlwind experience."

Through a combination of shrewd resourcefulness and
boundless energy, Kaile engineered his transformation from
a homeless person to the wealthy entrepreneur-owner of a
worldwide business. He is also a popular motivational
speaker and a home-improvement expert on CBS's *The
Early Show.* He did it one small step at a time. The morning
after his middle-of-the-night epiphany in the rat-infested,
abandoned warehouse, Kaile took the five hundred dollars
that he carried on his person—all that he had in the whole
world—and invested it in his idea. He had a phone installed
in a friend's building and had some fliers printed up that
said, "Need a husband? Obviously. Why not rent me?"
Then he went to the church where his old divorce support
group was meeting and put the fliers on the windshields of
the cars parked there. "The response I got from that was incredible," Kaile says, "and this was the first time that I
thought, 'This is pretty special.'"

Kaile's next move was pure shoestring showmanship. He
bought an old van for a hundred dollars from a local car
dealer, put the Rent-a-Husband® name on the side of it in

big letters with black electrical tape, and started driving the van around town, picking up work. An off-beat TV reporter pulled him over to the side of the road one day and said, "You know how many people have called my desk asking me to do a report on this Rent-a-Husband® truck floating around town?" After he heard Kaile's story and saw the warehouse he was still living in, the reporter did a feature on Kaile for the NBC station in Portland. Kaile likens the response to a Jerry Lewis telethon. "The phone just rang and rang and rang," he says. "I spent a couple hundred dollars making copies of that tape and sent it around to different TV shows. The Maury Povich people called, and the rest, as they say, is history."

Although Kaile would like to attribute his success to a brilliant mind, he feels very strongly that a lot of people could create an enterprise like his if only they were as open to change as he was. "There are a great many messages that you get from your intuition, and as soon as you're willing to listen to them and really adhere to them," he says, "the better off you'll be." He thinks that many people fall down on the adhering part. "Without passion and courage, all the intervention in the world is not going to do any good," he says. "What happened with me is that I got to a point where I lost all fear of anything. And I fear nothing any more. I don't fear death; I don't fear failure; I don't fear taking chances. That night in the warehouse I saw that my mission in life was to take the mundane job of being a handyman and turn it into something of a high art and a respectable career path for basically blue-collar-level workers. I'm working very aggressively and very intuitively to do that. All the many things that have happened with this company have been inexplicable, and that just reinforces to me that I'm doing the right thing with the mission that I have in front of me, and the mission in front of me is a true blessing."

Kaile's story represents the power of surrender—how your life begins to turn around as soon as you lift the massive burden of self-doubt off your back and rely on the help of a power much greater than yourself. Actually, you're putting your trust in a power much greater than your *image* of yourself, which, as we'll see, rarely does you justice. When you ask for "intervention," to use Kaile's word, you're transcending your perceived limitations and distorted thoughts that block out your awareness of all that you are.

The release of energy bottled up in negativity is so powerful that we perceive it as coming from a "higher power" than our normal selves or from an almighty being, for those who believe in God. Suddenly we're able to hear those messages from our intuition that couldn't get through before. An idea occurs to us that brings our past experiences together with our unacknowledged potential. The idea for Rent-a-Husband®, for example, seemed to pop into Kaile's mind instantaneously, but actually it had been brewing in his subconscious for a long time. When he was doing construction work, he was amazed at how couples would bicker with each other over household chores. He would sit at the kitchen table with a husband and wife, present a proposal to them, and watch their disagreements develop into a full-blown argument. "I always thought to myself, boy, if you could ever tap into that, you'd really have something," he says.

It wasn't until Kaile surrendered his lack of faith in himself that he was able to use his imagination to come up with a name and a marketing approach that tapped into his experience very aptly. The idea of renting a husband worked on the surface as a clever juxtaposition of seemingly incompatible words, but it also worked on a deeper level that was part of its magic. To most people, the word "husband" represents trust, security, and strength, and the idea of renting or having a short-term relationship with a service that had those qualities and could get the job done was very appealing to women. Kaile knew instinctively that if he could get the women to call and give him entry into the home, he would do a professional job, and sooner or later the men would call, too. In his moment of surrender, Kaile's past experience, his cleverness with words, and his flair for showmanship, none of which he had previously recognized, all clicked into place.

Feeling we have nothing left to lose gives us the freedom from fear to act on these ideas that come from deep inside ourselves when we're down and out like Kaile, but we don't have to wait to hit rock bottom the way he did. Whenever we do it, the act of surrendering to a power greater than our everyday concept of ourselves imbues us with the strength to persevere through hardship and create something meaningful from it.

Strange as it seems, thinking *too much* of ourselves, rather than not enough, is a big part of our problem with life—a major cause of the fear and anxiety that assail us when the unexpected happens. We think we should be able to make everything turn out the way we want it to, and when something upsets our fantasy of being in total control of the outside world, it unhinges us. We put more pressure on ourselves, try harder and harder, and end up working *against* ourselves.

> Thinking *too much* of ourselves, rather than not enough, is a big part of our problem with life.

Essentially, surrender means giving up your belief in your own omnipotence and turning over control of the out-

come of a situation to the limitless energy animating the en-
tire universe, call it what you will. You're not giving up control over yourself, only over the outcome; you're actually
gaining control over yourself by adjusting your thoughts
and actions according to circumstances, ultimately helping
you to reach the outcome you desire. You're like the driver
of a car with a battery that's gone dead. You can't restart it
yourself, no matter what you do. You turn the key in the ig-
nition and pump the gas a dozen times, and nothing happens. You're late for an important appointment, so you bang
your fists on the dashboard in frustration and curse and
scream—still nothing. Finally, you give up and call AAA,
and a man comes in a truck. He attaches wires from his live
battery to your dead one, gives you a jump shot, and you're
off and running. Not that the AAA man is God, but you get
the idea. You recognize that you need to ask for help, and
then you accept it.

The Power of Surrender

How does the dynamic of surrender work? It follows another law of the spiritual world, of which our physical
world is only a tiny, fractional, part, limited by time and
space and our five senses. When we remove from our situation all negativity—all our fears, doubts, anxieties, anger, recriminations, and sadness—we open up a space for the positive energy of the universe to come in and give us a new
lease on life. Carl Gustav Carur, an eighteenth-century
German doctor, scientist, philosopher, and painter, did a
moonlit seascape that is perfectly serene yet glowing with
energy at the same time, and wrote about it in a letter:
"When man, sensing the immense magnificence of nature,
feels his own insignificance, and feeling himself to be in

God, enters into His infinity and abandons his individual existence, then his surrender is a gain rather than loss."

That's the crux of the matter—giving up the idea that you alone hold the keys to your own salvation, a terribly heavy burden, and reconnecting with the infinite field of positive energy from which we all came. I think of that endless positive energy as the "Field of Answered Prayers," where all possibilities exist, including whatever it is you're fervently hoping will happen—recovery from an illness, getting over the loss of a loved one, having a happy family life, finding a great job, meeting a soul mate, achieving financial security, the attainment of some longed-for personal goal.

Once you connect to this positive energy field by surrendering the idea of your own omnipotence in the face of its awesome power, you attain an altered state of consciousness. Answers to your prayers beyond anything you could have imagined start to come into your life. You hear of an experimental medical treatment that works or you meet someone through a fluke and fall in love. Perhaps a job opportunity you never would have anticipated opens up or you have a flash of insight that completely turns your life around.

Our problem is our cultural conditioning. From childhood on we've been indoctrinated with the myth of the superindependent person as hero—self-reliance is glorified, and the person who relies on faith in the metaphysical world, the world beyond our five senses, is seen as looking for a "crutch." As a result, surrender has become synonymous with giving in or giving up. Through no fault of our own we've become so in love with the notion of our own grandiosity that it often takes a catastrophe to bring us to our knees. We pray and pray, and as soon as the worst has passed, we say, "Okay, God, I can take it from here." We go back to our old ways, thinking we're God instead of teaming up with God—and we revert to being a victim when our supposed omnipotence fails us. Once again, we're at the mercy of outside events to bring us down or buoy us up instead of maintaining that continual balance between serenity and energy that Carur captured in his painting.

How can you connect and stay connected to the Field of Answered Prayers when something happens that fills you with feelings of helplessness and despair? You need to break out of the claustrophobic box of self-involvement—your pain, your expectations, your fears, your frustrations—and offer love and support to other people who need help. Instead of closing yourself off from your family and friends because you're so preoccupied with your own troubles, give *even more* of yourself to them, and try volunteering to help strangers, too. "How can you ask me to help others when I'm in so much pain myself?" I hear you protesting. But helping others is not as altruistic as it sounds. It's unselfish and at the same time a very selfish thing to do, the kind of loving and caring response that gratifies the soul and gives you a wonderful feeling inside. We saw that in the aftermath of the terrorist attacks on the World Trade Center. All those police officers, firefighters, and volunteers helping to reduce the suffering of others reduced their own pain, too.

Thinking only of yourself makes your problems seem worse than they are, as if you're looking at them through a magnifying glass. You become all-consumed with them, dwell on them day and night, to the point where you can't relate to the other people in your life, much less connect with a metaphysical power that you can't even see. Your mind can only hold so much. The more space your ego occupies, the less room there is for your soul. To put it another way, the more you experience yourself, the less you experience something magnificent within yourself.

Please don't think I'm trying to minimize the seriousness of your troubles or the legitimate suffering they're causing you. On the contrary, I learned that certain events in life are too big to try to handle alone and how valuable it is to acknowledge our powerlessness to deal with them in comparison with the infinite power of the universe. Being full of ourselves disconnects us from that power and puts the weight of the world on our own shoulders. As soon as we admit our powerlessness to make the sun come up in the morning and go down at night and turn "fixing" what will happen over to some perceived entity greater than ourselves, we experience an enormous feeling of liberation. It's the freedom from the limitations of the self. The goal in life is not to know yourself but to know your soul.

There's no way to describe the relief I felt when I threw myself down on the bed in my room in Baylor Hospital

The goal in life is not to know yourself but to know your soul.

and surrendered control to God after hearing that my daughter had only a 10 percent chance of surviving her coma. Humbling myself before the greatness of God removed from me the crushing burden of responsibility for Rona's survival. Suddenly, I had the feeling that whatever happened, I would be given the strength to handle it. With that assurance, I was able to refocus my thoughts and energies on the present instead of obsessing about the future. I got up from the bed feeling freed of desperation and infused with resolve to help my daughter in every way humanly possible, knowing that a power much greater than myself would take care of the rest.

I thought of the power I surrendered to as God, an external entity, but it doesn't matter whoever or whatever your consciousness of a greater power is. You may perceive it as an entity within yourself secreted away in your unconscious. As long as invoking it lifts you beyond your normal perception of yourself, it will raise you to a higher level of functioning and bring about what we might consider to be miracles. Surrender your fear and anxiety and anguish—Who cares where they go?—and you'll find the resources instilled in all of us to fight our battles, the strength you never knew you had.

When something happens that tears your world apart, it's only normal to react with fear, anger, anxiety, confusion, and sadness. You automatically feel helpless and out of control, because some underpinning of your identity as a mature person—your family structure, your job, your physical well-being, your relationship with a lover—has been kicked out from under you. Suddenly you're thrown back into feeling the way you did as a child, before you developed the skills and strengths you have now. Feeling like a victim of events beyond your control, you think you're being punished unfairly, and you cry out, *Why me? Why me?* Your impulse is to push your pain away or search frantically for something to make it go away. But your automatic reactive impulses are victim responses, not the creative responses of a survivor, and you have to begin the process of transforming them as soon as you can.

Even while you are feeling the full brunt of your pain, hold firmly to the belief that you will somehow be better for this, and you will find gifts in this experience and give it meaning. The act of surrender helps put you in touch with your soul—the seat of your purpose in life—and hitches your creativity to the creative force of the universe. When you align yourself with that stream of infinite energy, whatever you're struggling to do becomes infinitely more attainable. Instead of flailing about on your own, you're moving along with the flow of positive, orderly direction that operates whole galaxies, keeps the planets from bumping into each other, maintains human life by governing the electrical forces between parts of the atom so they don't fall apart, and directs the billions of cells in our bodies to fight off disease and help us heal. Working in tandem with that kind of power certainly improves your chances of bringing about the fulfillment of the deepest purpose of your life.

Coming From the Right Place

Surrender will enlist the universe to help you with your problems, but only on one condition: You have to come from the right place. *The desire to benefit others has to be your prime motivation rather than your personal agenda.* Certainly you want some "goodies" for yourself, but that can't be *all* you want, not even the preeminent factor. You need to surrender wanting what you want purely for selfish reasons—to be successful only for the money and prestige, not because you're giving something of real value to people; a relationship so you won't have to be alone, not because you want to contribute to your partner's growth and happiness; recovery from an illness without concern for others who are ill.

"Answered prayers" happen only on a trial basis to see what you do with the answers. If all you care about is yourself, you may get what you want, but your success or happiness won't last. You'll eventually come up short, because selfishness is the wrong kind of energy to sustain anything or bring you lasting fulfillment, and you'll go chasing after the next thing and the next. But if you come from a desire to share with others, connecting with the Field of Answered Prayers, my metaphor for the flow of pure, positive energy "out there" and within yourself, will make what you create more gratifying. You'll be rewarded not only with the material things you want but also with a deep-seated feeling of fulfillment that no amount of self-centered striving can produce. I can remember a troubled period in my life long ago when I was frantically chasing after success with a television

"Answered prayers" happen only on a trial basis to see what you do with the answers.

pilot I had produced. The show was called *The New Woman,* and it featured women who were making waves in nontraditional roles either socially or in the workplace (one of my first guests was the head of The Mother Truckers, an all-female moving company out of New York). Although I thought the show could blaze new trails for women, that wasn't the real reason I was so impassioned about it. Deep down I was absolutely desperate to sell *The New Woman* because I had this intoxicating vision in my head of all the fame, glory, and power that would come to me as a television talk show host (I was definitely not coming from the right place). Several syndicators thought the show was a winner, but each time one signed on to sell it, something happened to jinx the sale—one man had a heart attack; another went bankrupt; a third had a sponsor back out at the last minute. After several years of riding this enervating seesaw of hope and disappointment, I finally gave up on the show, thinking, "There must be something better I can do to make a real difference in women's lives."

That was it—the transformation I had to make from self-concern to concern for others. Now I was coming from the right place, and I turned a corner into a new beginning that led to the most creative and rewarding work I'd ever done, work that eventually culminated in a career as a broadcaster. Who knows what would have happened with the TV show if I had put that kind of positive energy into it in the first place?

Surrender Versus Resignation

Surrender is not to be confused with resignation, a feeling of powerlessness that leads to depression and paralysis. Resignation is giving away your power; surrender is getting your power back. When you resign yourself to something, you believe there is nothing you can do. When you surrender, you have the faith that with the universe on your side, anything is possible. Surrender gets your creative juices flowing; resignation bottles them up. When you're resigned, you feel hopeless about everything and say, "What's the use?" But that's only a question, not the answer. Surrender motivates you to search for answers you can't even imagine when you're resigned. Your pain, fear, and anger don't go away when you surrender them, but you gain the strength to take all your outrage and sorrow and turn them into a resolve to make something positive come out of your experience. Loving more, deepening your compassion for those who suffer as you have suffered, is a way to ensure that the goodness of the human spirit will always triumph over tragedy and evil.

Let's look at examples of how resignation paralyzes and surrender

Hopelessness is only a question, not the answer.

empowers. Sarah was in her early forties when her fifteen-year-old son was killed in a traffic accident. Three years later her husband died of a heart attack. Although she had a nineteen-year-old daughter in college, Sarah felt her life would never be the same without her son and husband. She resigned herself to living a joyless life, rarely going out with friends because she felt she didn't fit in with her old social circle of married couples. Five years after her husband's death, Sarah still had no desire to date. She'd heard too many horror stories and didn't feel strong enough to face rejection. It occurred to her that if she went back to school for an MBA, she could get a much better job, but the idea of being a student again at her age didn't appeal to her. Even her daughter's wedding couldn't lift her out of the gray fog that had become her life. Although she was happy about the wedding, the thought that her husband and son wouldn't be there cast a heavy, dark shadow. Because Sara had resigned herself to feeling miserable, her pain had become a dead weight dragging her spirit down.

Georgia Nucci, on the other hand, responded with a completely different attitude after she lost both of her children in the same year. On January 2, 1988, her daughter, Jennifer, died at eighteen from hepatitis while she was an exchange student in Ecuador. Her son, Chris, nineteen, offered great comfort in dealing with the loss, telling his mother to remember all the wonderful and happy things about his sister and not to dwell on her death, because that would make a negative out of Jennifer's whole life.

Eleven months later, on December 21, Chris was returning home on Pan Am Flight 103 from England, where he was spending his junior year in a Syracuse University program, when a terrorist bomb exploded the plane over Lockerbie, Scotland. For about a month after each child's death, Georgia experienced the depths of grief, so viscerally painful that it felt like major surgery. But then she remembered what Chris said about concentrating on the positive, and she decided to help the families of the other Pan Am Flight 103 victims to focus on their happy memories, too.

She gathered family stories and photos into a commemorative book of profiles of those who lost their lives. She also became heavily involved in Victims of Pan Am Flight 103, a survivors' organization to lobby the government to solve the crime and to reform the way airlines deal with disasters. To fill the aching void left in her family and to make sure the terrorists weren't going to claim another victim in her by robbing her of motherhood, Georgia and her husband, Tony, decided to adopt a child in 1990. Georgia was forty-seven and Tony forty-nine, and they wound up with *four* children, a family group from an orphanage in Bogota, Colombia. Accustomed to working while raising her children, Georgia wanted to find a new career to replace her job as a real estate agent. That job had ended abruptly when her second child died and people in her community, superstitiously afraid she'd bring them bad luck, shied away from doing business with her. Rather than give up on a career and sulk the rest of her life, Georgia enrolled in law school at the age of fifty-one, and she is now a staff attorney for the New York Department of Taxation and Finance. "A lot of good came from those awful moments," Georgia told *Parade* magazine. "My life is fuller than it's ever been."

Fight or Flight

An overwhelming obstacle often triggers the fight or flight impulse our brains are wired with to deal with a perceived threat to our well-being. But this is a primitive response of the so-called "old brain," and yielding to it preempts your ability to deal with an outside event effectively. Flight takes the form of trying to escape from emotional pain into something that makes you zone out: alcohol, drugs, sex, food, a cult. But with these responses, you only experience a new kind of pain that comes from the loss of freedom over your own thoughts and actions. Fighting is similarly futile. When you fight a problem, you beat yourself up about it or lash out at the person who wronged you or shake your fists at God—all of which, like resignation, get you nowhere.

There is a third option: You can take control of your reactions, work to shape the kind of life you want to lead, and not let fate control you. Accept the present the way it is. Surrender all your expectations about it, and do all you can within your circumstances to strengthen yourself, not just for your own good, but for the good of the people who should be the basic focus of your life: loved ones, friends, community. That shift in consciousness from a reactive victim to a creative survivor will, without fail, point you in the direction of real, lasting inner peace.

Now we come to the Big Question: If, as many people believe, God is supposed to be all about infinite love and goodness, why do we have such dreadful things as illness, loss, natural disasters, accidents, terrorism, and death? That question was voiced again and again after the terrorist attacks on the Twin Towers, and I've heard it many times from people who were raised with religious beliefs and felt deeply disillusioned by some personal tragedy. One grieving mother asked me after losing her son to AIDS on his thirtieth birthday, "Is God a sadist?" No, I reassured her, the spiritual world doesn't work that way. These ordeals are not malicious punishments; they are tests of the human heart. They trigger our automatic reactions of fear, anger, grief, outrage, and despair, only to give us the opportunity to transform these negative energies into something positive for ourselves and others. I told the grief-stricken mother to resist the bitterness that was separating her from the great comfort she would find if she channeled some of her sorrow and anger into developing a deeper compassion for those who shared her suffering. She began working for an AIDS organization and found gratification that led her out of her cynicism and despair. Resolving not to be dragged down by an impulse to be self-involved and embittered, she surrendered instead to an uplifting force that led her to be more caring toward other people. In doing so, she found some inner peace and the strength to move on.

Even the little, everyday challenges of life that trigger our baser impulses—a disappointment or frustration that throws us into a temper tantrum, a delay that provokes our impatience, a disagreement that brings out our arrogance or meanness, the need to please that makes us afraid to speak our own truth—are tests to see if we'll succumb to our reactive impulses or surrender them and replace them with more caring or courageous responses. That doesn't necessarily mean that we should let people get away with rotten behavior. On the contrary, we need to help others resist their baser impulses, too—and that sometimes means being "tough" and setting limits. But even then we should come from a caring, not hostile and retaliatory place.

I believe that we are here on this earth for one reason only: to transform ourselves from self-centered into soul-centered beings. We start out as infants, crying and screaming to get our needs taken care of, and end up, it's devoutly to be hoped, as loving adults intent on contributing something to the world. Nothing gives us the opportunity to make that spiritual transformation like a challenge that pushes our buttons and forces us to rethink how we want to use the gift of life.

The following story demonstrates the valuable insights into oneself that come from complete surrender when tragedy strikes:

Kathy

At thirty-four, after a passionate and tumultuous five-year relationship with Greg, Kathy married him in a spectacular wedding given by her wealthy, socially prominent family on Philadelphia's upscale Main Line community. Less than a year later, early in the morning on July 4th weekend, Kathy and Greg were experiencing the joy of first-time parenthood with their nine-month son, Zack, lying in bed with them. Kathy was nursing Zack when she felt Greg's body suddenly turn rigid beside her. He'd stopped breathing. By the time she rushed him to the hospital, he was pronounced dead from a viral inflammation around the heart. In a literal heartbeat, Kathy's life had turned upside down, her joy vanished like a stolen treasure. "I was in shock," Kathy says, "so opened up from giving birth and then witnessing my husband dying. It was almost like Zack came in, and Greg left, like God took my husband away and gave me this incredible little baby boy."

A sweet, ethereal beauty as well as a deeply spiritual person, Kathy turned out to have iron in her gentle soul. "I was scared of being alone in this huge house we'd moved into right before Zack was born," Kathy says. "I was scared as a new mother to begin with, and I couldn't imagine how I was going to raise Zack by myself. I felt completely impotent, like all my strategies had been taken away, all my defenses, my ego, everything. All of my exits were gone, and I just had to give it over. I had no choice. There was nothing I could do, especially since I had a baby. I wanted to run and do a retreat, get on a plane and go to Bali, do Outward Bound, whatever. But I couldn't do anything. I had to sit and nurse my child. I had to be caught between the anguish and the pain of all that loss and the innocence of this new life and be a mother."

Kathy says she began to look on this period of grief as a "purification by fire" that put her in touch with her inner strength. In her words, "It was as if God said to me, 'Do you really want a test of your endurance? Okay, here's your Olympic opportunity.'" Surrendering completely to her misfortune and trusting that there was a divine plan for it dispelled any feelings of victimhood Kathy might have had and made her feel less helpless. She felt she just had to go down deep into her pain with no armor, because the best things come from visiting those dark places.

"It's tremendously cleansing to let the grief process happen and naturally run its course," Kathy says. "Not only are you grieving this situation but you really are grieving every grief you've ever had, and collective grief. I would just sob and sob for disaster victims I saw on the news, for the people in Chechnia and Bosnia, for people in other parts of the world living with oppression and poverty. There are waves, and you ride those waves. It started out that in a week I'd have maybe a couple hours of peace and seven days of despair. Then it would become six bad days and a good day. And then I'd have two good days a week. And then I started having a good day and then a grieving day, not a bad day, just a very sad day. It took its time, but sinking into it like that brought into sharper focus things about myself that I hadn't crystallized before."

One thing the grieving process made Kathy aware of was that not trusting her own strength enough and relying too much on other people's opinions had separated her from her true nature. "I always thought that somebody else had the answer or some *thing* had the answer," she reveals, "and nothing could fix this—nothing—there was no magic. I drew on my strength from my soul, and I got to see my own courage and my sense of optimism."

Kathy says she took that saying, "We plan, and God laughs" to heart. "I felt that there was a major reason for all this, that I wasn't being punished, and there was tremendous blessing that was going to come from it—I would become a much stronger person, and this was *making* me. I was going to come into myself."

And come into herself she did. In the depths of her suffering Kathy discovered a lesson in Greg's death—it broke up a pattern that she didn't want to repeat. Her whole life had been a struggle to carve out her own identity apart from the materialism and country club lifestyle that surrounded her when she was growing up, and yet in her marriage to Greg she was going down that very same path. "Moving into that enormous house with all the expenses and upkeep was what Greg wanted," she says. "I never wanted it, but I went along with it because I thought it was what I had to do to be in the relationship. Having Greg leave was the last thing in the world I wanted, but his death awakened me to the fact that I was giving away my power in the marriage."

"Every crisis is a choice point."

Kathy made up her mind that from then on she would consciously *choose* her life. She would pour her energy into raising her son and commit herself to one of her most uplifting passions—using theater to build peer support groups for teens in the school system. She also resolved that when she was ready to fall in love again, it would be with a man who shared her values. Five years after she lost Greg, she found that very man. "Greg's death tore my world apart and threw me back on myself unmercifully," Kathy says, "but I learned that there are no mistakes. Every crisis is a choice point. No matter what the situation is, if we just really choose, keep choosing life at every moment, then we'll prevail."

Strength-Building Exercise:
"Turning It Over."

It doesn't matter what your religious faith is. Even if you're an atheist or an agnostic, you can find immense comfort in turning over the emotions you're experiencing to a power greater than yourself, however you perceive that to be. The name you give it—God, the Creator, Divine Intelligence, Higher Power, the Universe, Fate—is not the issue (I use God as a code word for the pure, positive energy of creation). What's important is that you connect with this infinite, radiant energy and draw it into yourself to give you strength, solace, and inspiration in your time of need. Take advantage of it, and, like Kathy, you will find yourself converting your fear and despair into courage and optimism.

Prayer and meditation are very powerful ways to surrender your anxieties and other negative emotions to a source of positive energy and find support and a sense of comfort in a time of crisis. I want you to think of a brief mantra that epitomizes your complete surrender to a creative power with total certainty that this situation will work out and some important good will come out of it. For me, saying "It's in God's hands" reduced my terror about the outcome of Rona's coma—something beyond my control—and kept me focused on what I could do to help her. Some others you might try are:

- I turn everything over to you (or "You," if you believe in a God).
- What will be should be.
- I take refuge in you.
- I am open to unexpected blessings.
- Doubt cannot shake my trust in you.

- I know you will get me through this.
- I am letting go, because there is nothing to fear.

If you prefer, create one of your own statements of surrender or use a prayer from Scripture or any other source that appeals to you. Write it down and recite it or chant it whenever you feel in danger of being overwhelmed by your emotions.

Set aside some time for meditation and prayer every day, preferably in the morning before your day starts and in the evening before you go to bed. The length of time you spend is not as important as consistency—even five minutes a day can be very beneficial. Meditation, along with physical activity, such as walking or jogging, can benefit your body as well as your mind, reducing the effects of stress and converting your negative emotions into positive energies for your body.

Negative thoughts are like "soul static" on the line between you and your higher self—the major source of the fear, anger, guilt, and sadness that obstruct the connection and cause so much torment. It's much easier to shift your attention away from disturbing thoughts than it is to stop them. Meditation directs your attention away from recurrent upsetting thoughts to your breathing, a safe, natural focus for your concentration. Breath has been identified by many spiritual people as the movement of spirit in the body, a link between the physical and metaphysical worlds that connects us to all creation. By sitting still and trying to keep your concentration focused on your breath, you learn how to prevent your mind from wandering into negative thoughts that disconnect you from the source of all life and power. The more consistently you practice meditation, the easier it will be for you to gain control over your thoughts in times of stress.

One of the most basic and relaxing forms of meditation, one that brings body, mind, and spirit into harmony, is to sit in a comfortable position with your eyes closed and observe your breathing without trying to influence it at all. Just follow the cycles of your breath through inhalation and exhalation for a few minutes, focusing on the points at which one changes into the other. You might want to focus on inhalation as the start of each new cycle for a few minutes and then on exhalation.

Another breathing exercise that will help give you a sense of serenity is to imagine the universe blowing positive energy into you with each inhalation and withdrawing it with each exhalation. Lie on your back, close your eyes, rest your arms alongside your body, and focus on your breathing without trying to influence it. With each inhalation, feel the universe breathing love, support, comfort, and power into every part of your body, and try to continue this perception for ten cycles of inhalation and exhalation.

If you're good at creating visual pictures, you might want to buy a guided visualization tape and listen to the person giving you instructions on how to connect with your source of positive energy. However you do it, don't let a day go by without carving out some time to surrender the fears and worries that are occupying your mind and to express your absolute trust that everything is happening as it should for some ultimate good.

Prayer, meditation, and visualization are highly individual matters—there is no right or wrong way to do them—but they all involve complete relaxation of body and mind in solitude and being open to a powerful source of reassurance and calm. Use these tools routinely and with intense focus. The more often you drive out all the negative thoughts that consume you and create a channel for God to come in, love, and comfort you, the stronger you will become.

Here's a meditation/guided visualization I've used for people in crisis that you or a friend might want to tape record in a soothing voice, leaving enough time after each instruction to create the images and feelings you're being asked to imagine:

Sit in a comfortable chair, with your back straight, your feet on the ground, and your hands resting in your lap. Close your eyes and keep them closed throughout this meditation. Breathe in deeply and exhale through your mouth slowly, feeling all the tension and stress leaving your body, beginning at the top of your head and working down to your feet. Take a few minutes to release all your tension and let the soothing, loving energy of the spiritual world flow into every part of your body.

Now visualize that you're in a place filled with the awe and wonder of nature. You're a tiny speck gazing at a magnificent mountain range; breathtaking glaciers, a moonlit, starry night; a vast, calm sea. You feel you're in the presence of the power of creation itself, a force of abundance and endless giving, and you feel a channel opening up to connect you to that power.

Think of a specific problem you fear you can't handle, and communicate with the power of creation about it. Ask for relief from the negative thoughts and feelings your problem has aroused in you—anxiety, anger, grief, despair—and for the strength and wisdom you need.

Now feel a sense of power and confidence in yourself flowing into you from the creative energy of the universe all around you. Feel the certainty that with this power inside you, filling you with a desire to love and contribute to the people in your world, you will handle your problem.

Now imagine yourself acting with this feeling of supreme confidence and freedom from fear and all other negative thoughts and emotions within you. What is the first step you are taking to help yourself? What are you doing next? How are you relating to other people, and how are they relating to you? Let yourself take pleasure in your sense of power and your ability to love and contribute. Know that this creative energy is always within you, and you have the power to move through this challenging time to a new beginning in life, buoyed by that strength and confidence. See yourself resolving your problem, achieving your goal, healing from your physical or emotional wounds, finding happiness again, growing spiritually stronger through your power, your confidence, your love, and your contribution to others.

Slowly, on a count from five to one, bring yourself back to physical reality and reconnect with it, feeling yourself sitting in your chair and listening to the sounds around you. When you're ready, open your eyes, knowing that the creative power of the universe is always available to you and will support you as you move through your fear, doubt, and sorrow and begin to act with a heart open to unexpected blessings.

3

Old Lies/New Truths

In the aftermath of the worst terrorist attacks on America, many people said their fear and anger had given way to a persistent anxiety about the future, as if they were waiting for the proverbial other shoe to drop. Even after they returned to their usual routines of daily living, chilling thoughts kept creeping into their minds. What would happen next? Another horrific strike? Biological warfare? A nuclear attack? They knew that people in other parts of the world had grown accustomed to living with terrorism as a fact of life, but they never thought it would happen here. The sense of safety and security they'd always had was gone, and the world had become a different place. "Nothing will ever be the same," they said, and it was hard to convince them that whether our lives would be better or worse was up to us.

Some people gave in to their feelings of helplessness and vulnerability and developed a bunker mentality, scaling back their activities dramatically and experiencing a pervading sense of gloom. They had no plans to fly on an airplane any time soon, were staying away from malls and other places where large crowds gathered, and were afraid of riding the subway because of a biochemical attack. Although these people hadn't lost loved ones or suffered physical injuries in the terrorist strikes, they were victims all the same: Terrorism claimed their peace of mind.

Other people wanted the terrorists to know they weren't going to stop them from living a full life and being free. They were deeply saddened by the tragedy and worried about the future, as we all were, but they weren't going to let the specter of terrorism intimidate them or make them feel like helpless victims. They felt fear and acknowledged it, but instead of letting our normal human tendency to overestimate uncontrollable risks make them panic-stricken, they were fighting back like survivors. Uncertainty about the future, they realized, doesn't mean doom; it means learning to adapt. Not only were they taking airplane flights and mingling with crowds; at the same time they were taking practical steps to protect themselves and their families, like getting self-defense and security training and assembling survival kits for their homes. Although they were being careful, they refused to be cowed, knowing that law enforcement and intelligence agencies, the government, the military, and scientists were working around the clock to make our country as safe as possible—probably safer than it had ever been before the terrorist attacks.

Those who refused to be victims were also making their children feel safe by turning their minds away from hatred and violence and getting them involved in relief activities that gave them a sense of purpose and contribution. These people knew that lasting inner peace doesn't come from an outside event, no matter how gratifying, and can't be taken away by one, no matter how horrible.

Transcending Self-Doubt

You alone are the cause of your peace of mind; it can't come from any external happening or it won't be anything more than an ephemeral calm between storms. Uncertainty is a fact of life, whether on a global scale or in your personal world. As I learned from my daughter's accident, what you value most in life can be snatched away at any moment. That realization made me terrified to let my daughter out of my sight, even for a moment, after I first brought her home. But I knew that living in the shackles of constant fear and anxiety would have claimed a second victim of the accident—me—and I found a way to manage my fears rather than let them eat away at my enjoyment of life.

You can't eradicate fearful thoughts altogether, but you can transform them from chains that hold you back into a motivating force that propels you forward. It's a matter of breaking up old negative thought patterns and training your mind to think that whatever happens, you'll be able to deal with it. The outside event is not the enemy; it's your own self-doubt. Learn how to answer the nagging voice of self-doubt with absolute trust in yourself, as well as in the universe, and peace of mind will be yours.

The negative thoughts you have about yourself, filling you with fear and anxiety about your ability to handle any challenging circumstance, from beating an illness to recovering from the loss of a loved one to creating financial security, are not truths. They're nothing more than programming. In your childhood, you accepted as truths the critical judgments you received from a parent, a teacher, or some other authority figure, who often meant no harm or were themselves victims of self-doubt. You may have worked all of your adult life to dispel this damning litany of self-doubts, but when adversity propels you back into childlike helplessness, these old lies resurface with a vengeance.

If your parents were pessimists who looked at the world through a murky fog of misgiving, you might find yourself repeating these distortions to yourself, too, saying, "Things will only get worse." However you acquired this habit of mind, in your fragile state you let these lies about yourself and your prospects gather momentum and power, building and building, until you become immobilized by them. How do you break the spell these lies have over you? You stop telling them to yourself and create truths to replace them. The real truth, the one that sets you free, is the realization that the only power negative thoughts have over you is your belief in them.

> **The only power negative thoughts have over you is your belief in them.**

A crisis is a catalyst for a showdown between your voice of self-doubt and the voice of your higher self. I think of your higher self as the part of you that's connected to the positive energy of the universe and that sees you the way you want others to see you—with unconditional love and no judgment. It's as if you're on trial for your life, and your defense attorney (your higher self) has to make the case for you against the prosecutor (your self-doubt), who keeps characterizing you in the worst possible light. The best defense strategy for winning out over these recurring negative thoughts is to cancel them out with their opposites. Counteract every negative thought (*I can't go on, I'll never make it, I'm such a loser*) with a contradictory one emphasizing that you're a powerful, competent, and loving person who can find something of value in whatever happens to you in life. Focus your attention on evidence of your power, competence, and loving nature in other situations to prove conclusively that the voice of self-doubt is not to be believed.

Here's an example of how a crisis forced a man to reexamine an old lie from childhood and replace it with a life-affirming new truth:

Bill

At age thirty-six, Bill, a successful fashion designer, was diagnosed with the HIV virus. The son of an emotionally aloof military man and a repressed church-going mother, he found growing up gay in a small town in Nebraska an intensely isolating experience. "Homosexuality was something you just didn't talk about, least of all in my family," Bill says. "The only time the subject ever came up was when I was playing touch football at a family picnic, and my father ridiculed me for tossing the ball like a 'fag.' He had no clue."

When Bill was still in his teens, his parents' marriage broke up. His father moved out and was never heard from again. "I finally got up the courage to come out to my mother right before I went away to college in New York," he says. "She was horrified. She told me, 'You'd be better off dead.' She made me feel there was something radically wrong with me, that I was defective."

Even after Bill moved far away from his provincial hometown and created a wonderful life for himself, that deep sense of shame never left him. "I didn't feel I deserved to die of AIDS when I tested positive for HIV," he says, "but at the same time I felt there was nothing I could do to prevent that from happening, that it was somehow my destiny."

Bill began drinking heavily and became so depressed that he couldn't work. A friend suggested that he join a support group for HIV patients. "The people in that group were fantastic," he says. "Some of them were a lot worse off than I was, and yet they were upbeat and doing everything to help themselves. I'll never forget what one guy told me. He'd really been through the mill and was starting to make some progress on new medications. The side effects were rough,

but he took them in stride. 'On my bad days,' he said, 'I remember that I have AIDS—AIDS doesn't have me—and that
keeps me going.'"

In one of my seminars that Bill attended we did an exercise that got him to examine his outlook and challenge it. His
doctor had given him a good prognosis, so where was the
logic in all of his gloom and doom? There wasn't much, he
had to admit. He realized that his bleak attitude was largely a
function of his parents' telling him he was no good. He had
chosen to believe that, even though his accomplishments, together with friends who loved him, told him it was a lie.

I encouraged Bill to call his mother and tell her he was
sick, hoping an ensuing reconciliation would finally put the
lie to rest. He was very reluctant to do it, saying he expected
her to give him "a whole bunch of recriminations about my
so-called lifestyle" although he'd been with one partner ex-
clusively for twelve years until the partner had died of an
AIDS-related illness. But he called. And his mother surprised
him with how understanding and supportive she was. "She
became very emotional, telling me how much she loved me
and was proud of me for doing so well in my field," he says.
"I think she was afraid I might actually die, a kind of self-
fulfilling prophecy on her part, and she didn't want me to go
to my grave hating her." Bill credits his illness for bringing
his mother around. "If that hadn't happened," he says,
"we'd probably still be alienated from each other."

In all likelihood, Bill would still be alienated from *himself* if his illness hadn't forced him to confront his deep sense
of shame and refute the lies that shame had been telling him.
As soon as he began to create new truths for himself—that
he was a good person, that he deserved to live, that he could
control his illness—he cut down on his drinking and started
taking care of himself. His health improved. His mood

brightened, his energy returned, and he was soon back at work, confident that he had a long, productive life ahead of him.

Positive Thoughts Attract Positive Energy

Like the man who said, "I have AIDS—AIDS doesn't have me," never let your circumstances define you. You are not your circumstances; you have an identity that is independent from your circumstances and should not be thought of as synonymous with them. To think that because you've lost something, *you* are a loser is the hallmark of the victim mentality. If you have lost the ability to walk or speak normally because of an accident or illness, you are more than your crippled body. You are a person with a mind, a soul, a loving family and friends, and you have the capacity to enjoy many riches in life and set a course for yourself that brings you deep satisfaction.

Seeing yourself as the helpless effect of outside events is what triggers the reemergence of all of the old lies you've ever **You are not your circumstances; never let them define you.** heard or perceived about yourself. This leads to anxiety, depression, and getting stuck in your pain. Always remember there is a point deep within you—your higher self—that is not affected by your situation. Once you grasp this truth, you can use this point of wholeness and optimism to cast a new, more positive light on your situation and on your self-image. Freed of identifying yourself with your problems, you can face them objectively and drive out your fearful, depressing thoughts with positive thoughts that motivate you to function like a survivor.

If this sounds suspiciously like the power of positive thinking, it is. Critics like to deride positive thinking as simplistically smiley-faced, but studies have shown that people who try to be confident about their ability to get through crises successfully do rebound more quickly from setbacks than those who are burdened with self-doubt. There is even research done at the University of California, Berkeley, to suggest that maintaining a positive outlook may help *prevent* misfortune from happening to you. Interviews conducted over thirty years with women whose smiles were the most open and friendly showed that these women seemed to encounter fewer emotional and physical troubles. This finding is no surprise to me. It's consistent with the spiritual law that negativity is like a thick, impenetrable cloak blocking out the radiant energy of the universe, giving rise to indecision, uncertainty, and instability and eventually manifesting as illness, problems with relationships, financial loss, and worse. The people who are trusting and confident about their future create an opening for the energy of the universe: It can help them ward off adversity and recover from it when it does happen.

Your consciousness creates your emotional reality, and you control your perceptions, much the same as someone at the steering wheel of a car. To take your hands off the wheel is to invite chaos. Your thoughts race wildly ahead to problems that don't have to be dealt with this minute or imagined calamities that may never materialize. Negative thoughts, nihilistic or self-pitying, stir up painful feelings of anxiety and powerlessness and exacerbate a problem by drawing negative energy to it. In contrast, positive thoughts about your ability to cope attract positive energy into the healing process and shorten the time it takes to get through a crisis and come out the other side.

Like many children of overprotective parents, I grew up in a household where the smallest risk, like not wearing gloves in the winter, was tantamount to a death-defying act. Both of my parents were compulsive worriers, so it's no wonder that I spent a great deal of my life always expecting the worst and never giving myself credit for being able to handle whatever the worst might be. I was afraid of so many things—failure, being alone, sickness, losing my money, not getting the job, not being able to keep the job after I got it. Getting through the trauma of almost losing my daughter crystallized my thinking in another direction. Because the stakes were so high, I couldn't allow my fears to get the better of me. Whenever negative thoughts began their drumbeat in my mind—*she's not going to make it, I can't have a disabled child, I'm not strong enough do this*—I immediately countered them with positive ones that affirmed both her strength and mine. The remarkably calming effect on my spirit made antidepressants or anxiety drugs unnecessary. If I had any doubts about the efficacy of the power of positive thinking before that, they were gone.

The power of positive thinking is not a magic bullet. Like meditating (which draws attention away from anxiety-provoking thoughts), canceling negative thoughts out by putting attention into their opposites requires consistent practice. These negative messages you received in childhood have lingered in the recesses of your mind for a long time and may not be easy to dislodge. After you identify where they came from, it will take some hard work to marshal evidence to disprove and counteract them with liberating new truths. The exercises at the end of this chapter will show you how to do this. Commit yourself to them and practice them diligently every day until they become part of you. Besides getting you through this crisis, your new way of thinking will assist you at *every* turn in your journey toward a happier life.

Strength-Building Exercise: "Your New Truths."

The situation you're facing now is an opportunity for you to challenge hidden feelings of worthlessness or incompetence that often surface when someone is in the throes of a crisis. In this part of the exercise I want you to write down any negative thoughts you have about yourself, determine where these messages came from, and gather evidence to refute them one by one. For example, if you think you lack the energy to fight the battle you now have to fight, you might trace your lack of confidence in yourself to a teacher who used to tell you, "You're lazy." Now write down an instance in your life today that disproves this judgment and shows it's no longer true, for instance how hard you worked to complete a recent project or how much effort you put into activities with your children.

It may be some humiliating experience you had as child, rather than some cutting remark, that has left a permanent scar—inadvertently breaking a family heirloom when you were trying to help with the housework, being rejected for the sports team you had your heart set on joining, having your classmates make fun of you because you were going through an awkward stage. You might also have grown up in an emotionally unstable home or lost a parent at an early age, leaving you especially fearful of abandonment by a loved one. As a result of these experiences or the derogatory messages you received as a child, you might be telling yourself all kinds of negative things now that the fabric of your life has been ruptured in some way:

- I don't have any luck
- I can't do anything right
- I don't have what it takes
- I can't live without him/her
- I don't deserve to be happy

Refute these messages with examples that show they're untrue—occasions when you had good luck, things you did right, tests of skill or courage that you passed, areas of your life where you are able to function on your own and derive satisfaction, qualities you have that make you a worthy person. In other words, counteract these negative messages with positive ones you've received over the years. These are some questions to help you formulate a body of uplifting new truths about yourself that will transform your victim mentality into the outlook of a survivor:

- Did anyone ever make you feel special? What did that person find special about you?
- When did you realize you were good at something? What talents do you have?
- How much of any success you've had do you attribute to luck? How much to yourself?
- What have you done that you're most proud of?
- Who made you feel loved? How did they do that? What did they say?

However you phrase your new truths—*I can handle this, I am in control, I have strength and confidence*—believe in them as absolutes and repeat them to yourself habitually. They will make you aware that you have everything you need to get through this situation and benefit from it in the long run.

4

The Power of Talk

Have you ever stopped to think what defines us as distinctly human? It's the power of speech. No other forms of life can articulate their thoughts and feelings to another of their own species the way human beings can. Dogs and cats in their "secret lives" do communicate with each other in some fashion, we're told. But we alone have the ability to reach out to another person and express in words the hidden fears that haunt us, the sadness that wracks our souls, the anger that roils inside us when we're hurt. Words are the currency of comfort and the best protection we have against despair. Being able to lay bare our concerns to someone who listens sympathetically lessens the intensity of our burden, and that person may see solutions to our problems that we don't. Only speech, the ultimate expression of our humanity, has the power to reveal our innermost vulnerabilities and connect us to a caring human ear.

More Powerful than a Pill

In the month after the terrorist attacks of September 11, 2001, the use of prescription antidepressants by Americans rose by 26 percent, and a 16 percent increase occurred in the

Words are the currency of comfort and the best protection we have against despair.

use of antianxiety drugs and sleeping aids. Some of the people who were prompted to seek treatment after the attacks had prior but undiagnosed mental-health problems. But many others were otherwise healthy, except that they were stressed out about the tragedy and were experiencing normal human reactions to it. In spite of this jump in pill use, doctors found that many patients wanted conversation and counseling more than they wanted pills. This need to talk was particularly obvious at City Police and Fire Counseling Agency, the part of my mental health agency that treats police and fire officers and their families. For them, the loss of so many police and fire officers in New York was particularly devastating, but they were used to living with danger and knew the stress they were experiencing was not something that would disappear with a pill. Mainly they just wanted to talk to someone who offered caring for their loss and encouragement to find meaning in it—something you can't get from a pill. I'm not saying that drug therapy isn't necessary and useful in many cases, but conversation and connection are often more powerful agents of healing than anything yet discovered by science. This story told to me by Jason, a thirty-three-year-old man who nearly lost his leg in the 1993 terrorist attack on the World Trade Center and barely escaped with his life in the second one, demonstrates the enormous comfort talk can bring us.

Jason

"For the first week I was completely out of control," Jason says. "I kept having flashbacks of people screaming and dying all around me, and I couldn't get the horror out of my mind of crawling on the ground in pitch black darkness after some falling debris knocked me down. I was choking on the dirt and the awful smell. It seemed like the end of the world, and I was the last person left."

Jason's grief and panic persisted. He was afraid of going out, and every time he passed posters on the street of "missing" people, some of whom he recognized as coworkers he knew well, he would burst into tears. "I was a mess," he says. "I couldn't sleep or eat, I was jumpy, and I felt guilty that so many people in my firm lost their lives and I was still here." Jason knew from past experience that survivors who shut down emotionally and avoided thinking and talking about a disaster were likely to develop the most long-term psychological problems. He saw a close friend of his who'd also been badly injured in the 1993 bombing turn inward and resort to alcoholism, trying to forget.

"My wife, Vicki, is a nurse and very sensitive to people who are in pain," Jason says. "She tried to help, but I didn't want to lean on her too much, and we both decided that I should talk about my problems with a therapist. My first session brought me tremendous relief, just knowing that the posttraumatic stress I was suffering from was a common reaction, and I wasn't going to lose my mind."

As helpful as therapy was, Jason felt he wanted to talk to other survivors of the attacks in a more casual setting than a clinician's office. He wanted a feeling of camaraderie, so he began meeting with some of his colleagues and friends who'd been through the same experience. They shared their feelings, but they talked about them in a broader, more conversational way, and Jason found that the dialogue gave him a more objective view of things. "We were talking about our fears of what could happen in the future," he says, "and someone reminded us of how America got through other crises worse than this one before. There was World War II, where we were up against two major superpowers at the same time, and the Cold War that could have wiped out our whole planet with nuclear bombs. We were big enough and strong enough to survive that, so why couldn't we bring down a few thousand fanatics hiding in caves?"

Taking the long view of history made Jason feel more confident that our country would be able to stop the terrorists from committing another large-scale atrocity. He felt that this horrible event had actually made our world safer for his children and grandchildren. For one thing, it forced our government to protect us from terrorism more aggressively. And for another, it opened the door for our country to spread progress and modernization to other parts of the world so that extremism would lose its appeal to people living in desperate poverty, and its evils would become a sad footnote to history. "I stopped imagining what could happen tomorrow and focused on the big picture," Jason says. "I needed to get that kind of perspective to begin sleeping better at night."

The more Jason's group talked about their concerns, the more balanced their thinking became. They knew that other random attacks were likely to occur, but they became less consumed with fear about them as they gathered factual information and countered raw emotion with conclusions based on evidence and logic. "We tried to think in terms of probabilities," says Jason. "Statistically, what were the chances of one of us, or one of our spouses or children, getting hurt by a terrorist? We figured they were very low. Actually, the chances of getting hurt in a car accident were a lot worse, but that didn't stop us from driving."

When the Anthrax scare hit the news, Jason's group experienced new shock waves, and again they found that talking about the threat made it more manageable. "It was another thing to have to be cautious about," Jason says, "but it wasn't hanging over our heads. I guess what it comes down to is, terrorism is like all the other dangers that are out there—crime, disease, accidents, whatever. You have to guard yourself against them as best you can, but you still have to live."

Jason and Vicki understood that their children, nine and seven, needed to talk about their emotions, too, and be told that feeling scared, sad, and unsafe were reactions common to everyone, including their parents. Although some of the things the children were afraid might happen were the stuff of science fiction movies, Jason and Vicki were careful not to dismiss their fears as silly. "We just told the kids they were safe, and we would do everything necessary to make sure they stayed safe," Jason says. "We began spending more time with them as a family, partly to reassure them, and partly because the tragedy made us more aware of how precious they were to us."

Baring Your Soul

Whatever the calamity that tears your world apart, there is enormous comfort to be had in talking about it to someone who will listen empathetically—family members, friends, a therapist, a minister or rabbi, a support group, people at a community center or at your place of worship. Just as the act of surrender aligns you with a power greater than yourself, baring your soul to others in a time of crisis underscores the connectedness of all human beings. Sharing your inner turmoil with another alleviates your feelings of isolation, of being apart from the mainstream with no way to get back in.

Wanting to withdraw from people and be alone in troubled times, because you're trying not to think about your situation or might feel ashamed of what's happened to you or think you should be able to manage alone, is an invitation to victimhood. Any time you let your fears or your ego deny the needs of your soul, you short-circuit your growth. Your higher self wants you to seek unity with others, to find clarity and an objective vision, to grow stronger and not retreat from an opportunity for transformation into a protective wall around your pain that keeps it alive. None of us can do it alone.

None of us can do it alone.

Resilience research in recent years shows that disadvantaged children who managed to rise above the hardships of their youth had at least one mentor or caregiver—a grandparent, a teacher, a compassionate person in the neighborhood—who bonded with them. The ones who excelled the most belonged to a church group or club that provided some structure and stability. Seeking outside help when you're wrestling with a hardship is no less important for adults than it is for the young.

Paula is a perfect example of someone who wisely reached out for help in a situation that has driven over the edge others who've tried to handle it all alone. Right around the time when Leon, her husband of forty years, was diagnosed with Alzheimer's disease, a story hit the news about a man who became so distraught taking care of his wife suffering from Alzheimer's that he killed her. "That was all I had to hear," Paula says. "I thought, my God, what am I in for? We'd been looking forward to doing things together at this time of life with such anticipation, and now I was facing it with dread." Determined not to let herself be driven to desperate ends, Paula sought help from her local chapter of the Alzheimer's Association. "I met other caregivers there who took me under their wing," Paula says, "and I got a lot of information about the disease and some good tips on strategies for taking care of Leon as his illness progressed."

One thing Paula learned was that the caregivers who killed their spouses, and often themselves, were usually men. "I was told that men are more reluctant to ask for help or build a support network than women," she says, "and that struck a bell with me. It was so sad that the men who did this saw no other way out. Maybe if they hadn't kept everything to themselves, they could have persevered." Paula was committed to keeping Leon alive as long as she could but not letting herself get to the breaking point. "Friends I met at the Alzheimer's Association warned me not to be a martyr," she says. "They told me not to feel guilty if I had to pay for help so I could get out from time to time and take a walk, go shopping, get my hair done. I knew the money we set aside for trips would have to go into day care, because our health care system doesn't cover home health aides for more than just a few hours a month. And although I hated the thought of it, in the back of my mind I was prepared to put Leon in an assisted-care facility when the time came."

For the next fifteen years Paula endured the heartbreak of watching her husband, once a successful accountant with a lively, facile mind, slowly unravel into a second infancy. She went through it all—the withering loss of companionship and a social life; the exacting days and sleepless nights of being on full alert every second; the utter physical, mental, and emotional exhaustion; the relentless financial drain. Paula held out as long as she could, but when she felt it was too dangerous to take care of Leon at home alone any more, she placed him in a care facility. At the very end, she brought him home to die at eighty-one. But Paula never forgot how the Alzheimer's Association prepared her for that long, dark journey and gave her the strength to go through it. Now a volunteer for the organization, she is counseling caregivers struggling to keep their heads above the water and is holding out the same lifeline to them that once saved her from drowning in despair.

Paula's story emphasizes how important taking care of *oneself* is for any "well spouse" thrust into the role of being a caregiver to a partner disabled by an accident or a debilitating disease. Talking to supportive people reduced the guilt Paula felt when she took time for herself or made the decision to put Leon in a facility. We're supposed to grow spiritually from a hardship, not destroy ourselves proving we can handle it. People shouldn't be labeled callous or selfish if they know in their hearts that they can no longer take care of a loved one by themselves at home and choose to put that person in a facility. These people are no less spiritually evolved than those who work ceaselessly to take care of an incapacitated person by themselves. No two people have the same amount of stamina or the same relationship with a spouse. The ones who devote themselves to being a caregiver day in and day without end are

> **We're supposed to grow spiritually from a hardship, not destroy ourselves proving we can handle it.**

not saints nor are the others sinners—they are both human beings trying to do the best they can with what they have.

Pulling Back From the Point of No Return

One snowy day in Philadelphia, when many people were stuck inside their homes and a pensive stillness seemed to have settled over the city, I thought it would be a good time to ask the listeners to my radio show to call in with their true confessions. I was amazed at how many grown people were still haunted by childhood sins like snitching money from the collection box at church or returning a chocolate to a box of candies after they'd pushed their thumb through the bottom and tasted it. Of the more serious confessions, there was one that left a deep impression on me. A man recalled an incident that happened years ago when he was getting into his car to go to work one morning. A neighbor of his came up to him and said, "If you have a few moments, I'd like to talk to you." But the man was in a hurry to get to work and told his neighbor he'd get back to him later after he got home. Unfortunately, he didn't get the chance. "When I got home, there were police cars in my neighbor's driveway, and I learned he committed suicide," the caller confessed. "All this time I've felt remorse, wondering if I could've saved the man's life if only I had stopped to talk to him when he wanted to."

Suicide has been on the rise for a while, and there could be a big upsurge in it if people affected by the World Trade Center tragedy don't talk about their feelings and get help before their hopelessness becomes overpowering. Children are highly vulnerable, especially those whose mother or father kissed them goodbye in the morning before they left for work and never came back. Even before the terrorism attacks, suicide was the second-leading cause of death in America for teenagers between the ages of fourteen and nineteen, and the rate for children ages ten to fourteen had tripled in the past decade. Although a leading cause of death, suicide is often preventable, particularly so for people who think they can't go on because some adversity has made them feel desperately isolated and hopeless about the future. These suicidal people want to live but have lost the capacity to think clearly. Talking about their suicidal thoughts will not cause them to commit suicide—the opposite is true. Like the neighbor who tried to talk to my radio show caller, if suicidal people don't talk to someone about their problems and get a different perspective, they may succumb to the sinister impulse to take their own lives.

Many of the people I talked to who lost loved ones in the 9/11 terrorist attacks told me they were troubled at first by thoughts of suicide. This was their first experience with such profound loss, and their immediate reaction was an intense desire to join the person they had lost, because they couldn't imagine life without this loved one. Although they knew in the back of their minds that they would never carry out their thoughts of suicide, they were frightened by them nonetheless and thought they were going crazy. It was comforting for them to find out that thoughts of suicide and other irrational thoughts are normal in the early stages of grief. After Rona's accident, I had thoughts of suicide and even homicidal thoughts of killing the drunken driver who caused it. I scared the hell out of my husband when I talked about these thoughts with him, but talking about them helped me realize how irrational they were and how much I still had to live for.

Fortunately, the suicidal state usually lasts for only a short time—a few days or a few weeks at the most. In that crucial time a person who is thinking about suicide can be pulled back from the point of no return by talking about these thoughts to a caring person and getting help. Our thoughts create our reality. When we dwell only on what we lack—our lack of a loved one, our lack of acceptance by our peers, our lack of financial security, our lack of good health—we create a life not worth living. Negative thoughts overtake the mind, and we temporarily lose our ability to change our perspective on our problems and see them and ourselves in a more optimistic light. Our ability to recognize distorted perceptions for what they are and replace them with positive truths, described in the previous chapter, has shut down. We need to be alert to signals that this has happened in ourselves or in someone close to us so that we can talk about these destructive thoughts and reorganize them into a more promising reality.

If you are the sur-
vivor of a loved one who   **Our thoughts create our reality.**
has committed suicide,
be aware that not all suicides are preventable, especially if the person has a chronic mental illness and is not helped by prescribed drugs or doesn't take them. It would be no more reasonable for you to blame yourself for a person's intractable death wish than it would be to hold yourself responsible for someone dying of terminal cancer. Some suicidal people take their lives without giving any overt warning. Anger, at the deceased or oneself, and guilt are normal reactions, but the question, "Why wasn't your love for me enough to keep you from leaving?" is like the universal "Why me?"—a cry of pain. The only answer is to transform your anger and sorrow into an understanding of the illness that caused the person to commit suicide, forgiveness of the person, compassion for others who are suffering like you, and a deeper appreciation of the gift of life.

The Good Listener

"I thought I was going crazy until I talked to you." That was something I heard many, many times from the women who called Wives Self Help, the nonprofit hotline I started in the 1970s for people experiencing trouble in their marriages. The relief of the anonymous caller on the other end of the line, after revealing the secret, sometimes shocking circumstances of her marital life and unburdening herself of the pain she felt because of them, was almost palpable. It was clear that the woman struggling in private with her marital problems desperately needed someone to talk to, without making herself vulnerable to gossip or moral judgment. I think she was half expecting the listener to faint dead away, rebuke her, or hang up the phone after hearing her story. Instead, she was enormously grateful to receive a comforting word, the reassurance that she was not alone, some practical wisdom born of experience, and referrals for further help. After many years of doing this work, I had the sense that what people need, almost as much as food and oxygen, is the irreplaceable comfort of the so-called sympathetic ear.

Before Wives Self Help sprang into being, for years I'd been one of a tiny network of friends spending long hours on the telephone giving each other aid and comfort during hard times in our marriages. We cried with each other at the more painful things, laughed at the more absurd ones, vented our anger and frustration, and revealed secrets we didn't feel comfortable telling anyone else. What a relief it was! Our telephone dialogues, with their mutual exchange of sympathy, insights, and common-sense advice, played a pivotal role in sustaining us through the agony of trying to save our marriages or summoning the courage to get divorced. We realized there must be other people out there hurting just like us who had no one to talk to, and we decided that if our kitchen brand of counseling had worked so well in our own small circle, why not extend it to the community at large? We didn't intend it to be a substitute for professional therapy, only a kind of emotional first aid for a woman who was just gathering the courage to bring her troubles out into the open. For someone in that initial stage, talking to an empathetic, experienced peer was a safe middle ground between suffering in silence and deciding to see a therapist. Today, in addition to support groups, there are hundreds of Internet Web sites and chat lines for people coping with every kind of crisis. They are a testament to the truth I discovered long ago—there is no comfort for a soul in pain like being listened to by a soul in sympathy.

The suffering you experience can be even more intense if your marriage ends because your

> **There is no comfort for a soul in pain like being listened to by a soul in sympathy.**

spouse has died. Having someone taken from you forever can cause intense anger—sometimes misdirected at God or at the person who is gone, but mostly a kind of blanket anger at the whole world. You're angry about the loss of companionship that everyone else seems to have. If you have young children, you're angry because the person who was supposed to help you raise them and was such a huge part of their lives is gone. You don't know how to console your son because his father won't be there to see him play on the football team, or you don't know what to say to your daughter when she cries, "My daddy will never see me go to the prom or walk me down the aisle when I get married." As an older woman looking forward to retiring with your husband now that your children are grown, you're angry because you feel completely adrift, without any structure or sense of direction. And if you're a man, you're angry because you're wife wasn't *supposed* to die before you, and you're angry at yourself because you think you should be strong and keep quiet about how much you hurt.

What do you do with all this anger? If you don't express the rage you feel, it will turn inward against yourself and intensify your depression. But when you talk about your emotions to family members and friends, you may find that some of the people you were counting on for solace don't want to listen. They may feel uncomfortable around someone in so much pain and try to change the subject, and your married friends may start avoiding you because they feel, irrationally, that losing a partner might be contagious. Some people simply don't know what to say or are afraid that talking about your loss will depress you. You can make it easier for them if you tell them you need to talk about your loved one and share memories with them. Find family members or friends you can trust or a therapist who will let you pour out your feelings without restraint. Web sites and chat lines for widows and widowers are another source for catharsis, and support groups that meet regularly provide some sense of structure and an opportunity to form friendships with others in the same situation.

The death of a child is a profound devastation unlike any other in the wild force of its blow to the heart. Who better can empathize with the depths of your pain than other bereaved parents? Their support in the early stages of your grief can be invaluable.

Finding the Right People

As indispensable as connection and conversation are, you have to find the people who relate best to you and the surroundings where you feel most comfortable. Kathy, the new wife and mother in Chapter 2, whose husband died suddenly in bed next to her while she was nursing their baby, cringes when she remembers how upsetting some would-be comforters were to her. "Everyone was so morbid, telling me how horrible it was," she says. "Then there were others who treated my husband's death like a social event. A friend of his showed up at my house the first week and took business calls the whole time she was there. Having people back to the house after the memorial was horrid—loads of sandwiches everywhere, people gabbing about the house—everything was ludicrous to me, bizarre, chaotic."

Support groups were no better for Kathy. She went to one that a group of older women had formed in her community. There were about fifteen to twenty women, all about twenty years older than Kathy, and two bereavement counselors. "The counselors told us to go around the room and take turns telling our story, about ten minutes each," Kathy recalls. "Everybody was just going at it, almost trying to outdo each other, and it turned into a 'Can you top this with your grief?' kind of thing. They went on and on and on, and when they got to me—I was one of the last— they said, '*But yours is the worst!*' I didn't find it very helpful at all."

What Kathy did find helpful was being with her parents and their friends, people with whom she didn't have to put on any pretenses and who made her feel she was surrounded by a lot of extended family. "It was good to have dinner out and be in a social environment where I didn't feel I had to keep up with my peers," she says. But she did have some "amazing" friends, one a single woman who lived with Kathy for three months, just to be there with her and her infant son, Zack. "Friends of mine came in from all over and gave me a tremendous amount of support," she says. "They knew my husband and were really feeling the loss, too. They sat on my bed while I was nursing Zack, and with them I could cry all I wanted and talk my feelings out. I needed people, but it had to be the right kind of people, people who let me grieve and be myself."

Forcing yourself to find the "right" people after you've lost a loved one or have suffered any devastating adversity is worth the trouble. Besides providing emotional support, social interaction on a regular basis imposes some structure on the chaos that a misfortune brings in its wake. Falling into the pattern of sleeping 'til noon and mindlessly watching television the rest of the day is poisonous. That kind of self-imposed isolation where the only goal is numbness prevents you from taking your first baby steps toward getting back on your feet. Whether it's meeting with a support group, going to the gym, taking your children to school and back every day, keeping up as normal a work schedule as possible, you need anchors, regular activities you can count on to stabilize you. Volunteering to help others in need—at a disaster site, at a food bank for the poor, at a senior citizen's home, at a homeless shelter, at an orphanage, at a center for disadvantaged youth, at a pet shelter—is one of the most gratifying ways to give you a sense of connection and belonging in this period of flux and uncertainty.

Your feelings of dislocation may tempt you to respond with more dislocation—selling your home, uprooting yourself and moving away to start over somewhere else. In time this could very well be the right course of action, but for now, maintaining as much stability as possible will help you feel grounded at a time when you seem to be flying out in space with no supports. Keep reaching out to others, opening yourself up to them and inviting them to share their concerns with you, and you will find that no matter how alone you feel, you are *not* alone. As comforting as your religious faith or beliefs may be, on an everyday level there is no greater comfort than having someone hold your hand and walk with you through the dark.

Strength-Building Exercise: "You Are Not Alone."

Everyone needs someone to talk to during times of high stress and emotional pain. Take charge of building a support network that is most appropriate and comfortable for you. Some of the resources that people find most helpful are:

- Empathetic family members and friends
- Support groups
- Social or religious organizations
- Internet Web sites and chat rooms
- Therapists
- Clergy

Make finding yourself the right source of help a research project. If you think talking to a therapist would be beneficial for you, ask your doctor or friends who've been in therapy for recommendations, or call the psychiatry department of a local hospital for referrals. To find a support group, read your newspaper for notices of meetings in your area, call religious or social service agencies in your community, contact organizations dealing with a particular illness or situation, start your own group of others in the same situation, or look on the Internet.

Support groups are available for people facing every kind of adversity—widowed people, caretakers, bereaved parents, people with a serious illness or disability, or those coping with suicide prevention or survival. Use all the resources at your command to find the right one for you, but remember, as Kathy pointed out, support groups are not for everyone. If you feel uncomfortable or unsatisfied with the one you've chosen, drop out and try another group or a different kind of resource altogether. The important thing is not to isolate yourself and to reap the benefits of emotional support and practical information that are vital for coping effectively.

If you've been fired or laid off, networking is the most fruitful method for finding a new job. The wider your circle of contacts, the more likely you are to find reemployment. Stay in touch with family and friends, try to make new friends, and meet regularly with other job-hunters to lend each other encouragement and share leads and strategies. Bear in mind that only 10 percent of people find jobs on the Internet, so consider other alternatives as well. Look for resources in your area like the Consortium for Worker Education, which runs New York's Worker Career Centers. The organization has provided job training and counseling for 12,000 people and is geared up to help many thousands more who are unemployed because of the World Trade Center disaster. Be open to putting your skills to a new use in a different sector of the job market or to developing other aptitudes you have but have never done professionally.

The second part of this exercise has to do with maintaining as much structure as you can in this chaotic time. You need to arrange temporary structures while you're regrouping from a shattering of your old ones—getting a temporary or volunteer job while looking for a permanent one, for example, if you've been fired or laid off. Kathy was fortunate to have a friend stay with her for three months while she was nursing Zack, but there are other kinds of arrangements that can be made to avoid becoming depleted in the aftermath of adversity.

Whether it's hiring help at home, as Paula did when she was taking care of Leon, her husband suffering from Alzheimer's, or cutting back at work because you've suddenly become a single parent, you need to find time to take care of yourself in little ways. Get away for a day of sheer relaxation by yourself, see a movie, exercise, have dinner with friends. Explore every means of conserving your energy for the crucial inner work you must do on your journey toward resilience and transformation.

Part II

Reflection

5

Acceptance Means Letting Go

I love to watch plants grow, shedding their fat, tired, old leaves, discolored with age, and sprouting vital baby leaves, shiny and bright green with promise. It's a metaphor for the way we grow internally as human beings. To stay alive and healthy as we keep expanding our dimensions, every so often we need to let go of a familiar part of ourselves that has outlived its usefulness and create something new. Some people make internal changes quietly of their own accord, and others have change violently thrust upon them by outside events. Theirs is the more difficult path of loss and regeneration, but those who resist change, who can't let go of anything, cease to bloom.

In the first stage of resilience—the Rupture Stage immediately following the impact of a calamity—your primary purpose is to absorb the pain without letting yourself wallow or drown in it. You keep yourself afloat by taking these steps to gain control over your fearful, angry, or grief-stricken thoughts and feelings:

1. You accept the disruptive event as an opportunity for transformation.
2. You surrender your fears about the outcome to

a power greater than yourself.
3. You silence your self-doubts with positive
   thoughts.
4. You reach out to other people.

There is no timetable for going through these initial steps of the grieving process, and you can't compare someone else's loss to yours. A man I know, who was the father of six children, was as devastated when his wife lost their seventh in childbirth as he might have been if that was his only child. Some people can function after severe loss, and for others it can become incapacitating. According to an article in a 1991 issue of the *Journal of Marital and Family Therapy* by clinicians who learned about grief from normal families, substantial incapacity can last anywhere from nine to fifteen months after a miscarriage, one to three years after a child dies, and three to twelve months after losing a job. These adaptive steps that help assuage your feelings of helplessness and isolation will shorten the grief process and make it more bearable. Although some of your intensely painful feelings over the loss of a loved one may come back at certain times, like holidays or family events, your pain will lessen over time. Grief is not a permanent state; it's a transition between being stricken by loss and integrating the experience of loss into your life. As you go through this next stage of Reflection and on to Rebuilding and Regeneration, you not only will return to your normal level of functioning but will function even more effectively than you could before.

Doing a Life Review

Now that the shock and emotional turbulence have subsided, you've entered the second stage of your journey, the

Reflection Stage, a time for you to accept your loss by letting go of the image you had of yourself before this event happened. Once you were a spouse, now you're widowed or divorced; once you were a parent to a child, now that child is no longer here; once you were employed in a particular job or career, now you're unemployed; once you were in the peak of health; now you're sick or disabled. The love that you had with a spouse or a child or a sibling who has died will always be with you in memory and in your heart, but you have to let go of the part of your identity that was tied in with that person. Some phase of your life has ended, and now you must let go of the way you defined yourself then—not just outwardly in the way you presented yourself to others but also in terms of your beliefs about yourself and the world—and prepare yourself for a new beginning.

This is a time for reassessment—a life review, so to speak, as you position yourself to make that new beginning. What is your real purpose in life, the main reason you are here? What changes do you have to make in your outlook, your beliefs, or habits that will bring you closer to achieving that purpose? If you were part of a couple and now you're alone, what beliefs about yourself do you need to let go of so that you can create fulfillment in your life without a partner? If you were healthy and now you're sick, what habits do you need to let go of that have compromised your health? If you were working, and now you're out of a job, what attitude or goal is it time to let go of that could be holding you back? You've been shaken loose from your moorings, but this uncertainty is brimming with freedom of choice. This rootless period is a chance to go deep inside yourself and figure out what you need to let go of internally before you can begin to move forward again.

Becoming a More Authentic Person

You may have lost someone or something you thought you could not live without, but this is an opportunity for you to find a new purpose for living. Transformation is an ongoing evolutionary process, the whole point of which is to bring your self-concept into closer alignment with your soul. The difference between the two is this: Your soul is you without your story. Your self-concept is the composite of your beliefs about yourself, mostly arrived at by unreliable input from people in the outside world. It's the story you tell yourself about who you are, based on your relationship with others. Your soul, on the other hand, is about your relationship with yourself. It's not your ideas about who you are; it's who you *actually* are, the real being you were in your original state as a particle of the pure, positive energy of the universe.

Your soul is you without your story.

Your self-concept always keeps you on the defensive, guarding against the loss of your role or the external trappings you have that make you feel comfortable and give you status in other people's eyes. Your soul urges you to expand and discover hidden attributes within yourself or changes you need to make as it leads you along an upward spiral toward wholeness and happiness based on your deepest values. The soul is what makes a dentist walk away from his profession and become an artist or a media executive leave her high profile job and become a psychologist. The work they were doing, fulfilling as it is for some people, fed their self-concept as a successful achiever but left them cold inside. They needed to find other work that made them feel they were being who they were meant to be.

Repeating the Past Is Not a New Beginning

It doesn't matter whether you decide to let go of what you have or whether it's taken away from you unexpectedly; your letting go of it in the fullest sense is essential. It's not only the job or the relationship you have to let go of but everything attached to it—the role you played in that job or relationship, your daily routines and preoccupations, and all the hopes and dreams and worries you had about it. If you don't let go fully, you'll just be transferring the past into a different situation instead of making a genuine new beginning. You'll be one of those people who keep changing jobs or relationships but can't find fulfillment because they bring all of their old "baggage" with them wherever they go. If you've lost a loved one, you will remember and love that person as long as you live, but you can't focus on the past or you will drown in memory.

Clinging to your old self-concept will make you keep hounding yourself about what you've lost and how to replace it quickly, and you won't give yourself the breathing space to find answers that support your growth. The way you dealt with other people in the past may not work for you now; the values you held most dear then may have lost their appeal. The Reflection Stage should be a "time-out" between the end of your old way of being and the creation of a new one, a period of quiet gestation of ideas about how to emerge from your loss as a more authentic person.

Without the job you used to go to every day or the person you used to go to bed with at night and wake up with in the morning, this dormant interim looks like a terrifying void in your life. It seems so vacant, formless, filled with nothing but confusion and uncertainty, the blank space inside the curve of a question mark. But don't let this apparent emptiness fool you. Like the gestation period in pregnancy, nothing is visible on the surface yet, but a lot is going on inside. Although recovery is the word most often used to describe bouncing back from a loss, what you're actually undergoing is a rebirth. Our inner lives evolve kaleidoscopically. At every turning-point in our development, we're forced to cast aside something that doesn't fit us any more—some belief, attitude, or goal—like a child who outgrows his clothes or progresses from a tricycle to a two-wheeler. But we don't jump from one way of being to the next overnight. Much as it goes against our reactive impulses to do something, *anything*, to get back what we lost, we need to suspend activity temporarily and let our creative ideas for solutions simmer and take shape.

Letting Go After You've Been Let Go

In these days of economic downturn, learning how to brave the space between the loss of one job and finding the next one is becoming an all-too-common challenge. If you have a mortgage to pay, children to feed and clothe, and college tuitions looming on the horizon, you may think you don't have the luxury of a quiet period of reflection. The loss of structure in the gap between the end of one phase of your working life and the beginning of the next provokes intense anxiety, too. But you have to remember that structure is all you've lost—you haven't lost your life. Prematurely rushing out to find a clone of the job you lost may have more to do with the fear of the unknown than with any practical considerations. Your reactive impulse to repeat the familiar will always put up a powerful resistance to your creative urge to grow and will keep you stuck in an outgrown pattern if you let it.

Walter, a forty-two-year-old father of three, learned that repeating a role you thought was

Structure is all you've lost— you haven't lost your life.

right for you at one stage of your life without exploring whether it meets your deepest needs now is a mistake. When a management shakeup cost him his job as marketing director at a technology company, Walter couldn't let go of his image of himself as a successful executive and immediately went searching for the same position at a different company. "I had a lot of stress on that job—I packed on forty-five pounds and developed high blood pressure during the five years I held it—but I didn't want to switch horses in midstream," he says. He felt a sense of urgency, if not panic, about finding work soon. "My wife had been laid off from her job right after we moved into an expensive new home," he explains, "and our seventeen-year-old son was about to start college."

After three months of job-hunting, Walter thought he was lucky when another technology firm hired him as its director of marketing. "The responsibilities were pretty much the same," he says, "but it was a smaller company, and I thought the stress would be more manageable." Much to his disappointment, it wasn't. Walter soon found that despite his new surroundings and the different personnel, he still felt suffocated by the job, as if he were being buried alive in a daily landslide of paperwork and staff meetings. He was replaying his old managerial pattern in a new environment, and it was becoming apparent to him that he needed a change.

"People told me I was crazy to quit my job after less than two years without another position lined up," Walter says, "but I felt I would explode if I didn't get out and take my chances. It's very frightening to leap out of anything without knowing where you'll land, but the worst fear of all is that you're wasting your life."

Away from the pressures of his daily routine, Walter thought about what he wanted his career to be like several years down the road, what kind of work he cared about and wanted to be doing. "This time I wanted my job to be a conscious choice," he says. "My first marketing director's job came about almost as a fluke. I was a Web site developer at the company, and my work caught the attention of the head of human resources. I became friendly with him, we went out socially together, and when the marketing director's position opened up, he asked me to take it."

Walter found the salary and the idea of being in a position of some authority enticing, but he was never passionate about being a manager the way he was about developing Web sites. He decided that it was the creative side of the business that brought him the most satisfaction, and he went back into it as a freelancer. "I wondered whether my decision would make me look like a failure in some people's eyes," he says, "but that only lasted a minute. You have to define success on your own terms." Walter's family was prepared to scale back their lifestyle while he built up a client base, but that happened faster than he expected. Today he is healthier and more productive than he was in his old job, and feeling happier than he has in a long time. "People think that courage is hanging in and toughing it out," he says, "but sometimes what you really need is the courage to let go."

In my career as a radio talk show host I learned how important it is to let go after you've been let go. Transience is the trademark of this field. Program directors come and go through a revolving door, and each time a new one comes in, people who are currently working at the station are pushed out. I've been fired twice in my life, both times because the radio station I was working for changed its format. The first time was devastating. I'd been working at the CBS station in Philadelphia for eleven years and had built up a loyal following who were more like family than listeners. I started out as a commentator on women's issues; then got a weekly advice show called "Changing Your Life"; and finally became the host of a daily three-hour talk show covering everything from local and national politics to arts and entertainment.

For four years I interviewed famous, fascinating people and engaged in a dialogue with listeners from all walks of life on the issues that struck an emotional chord. At the end of the fourth year I heard rumblings that the station was seeking a younger audience. One day, without warning, a new, young program director called me into his office and told me that, along with the morning man, I was history. I felt a cold chill creeping up my arms when I heard this news. It was like being blindfolded, led down the hall into a room, and shot in the head. My life as a media personality had come to a quick, cruel end.

Or so I thought. Three weeks later I was hired by a much smaller station at a fraction of the salary I'd been making. It was a letdown, to be sure, but at least I was still clinging tenuously to my status as a talk show host. I was growing increasingly frustrated with the station's small audience and weak broadcast signal when a talent agent called me up out of the blue and asked me if I wanted to come to New York and do a show there. Did I! This was my fantasy, the dream that had kept me going through the humbling year and a half of working at a station below the radar screen. The agent got me a week-long audition filling in for a vacationing host during the Christmas holidays. At the end of the first week, the program director asked me to do another week. Six months later I was hired to host my own daily show.

I arrived in New York, filled with dreams of glory, only to find a Catch-22. Instead of doing a show that would appeal to the broad spectrum of listeners, the general manager wanted me to do a show strictly for working women—only they couldn't listen to it because they were working when it was on.

I felt stifled by this format, but I carried into this new job the same reluctance I had to speak up for myself to management when I was working for CBS. You can stay in the same field and grow, but not if you bring your bad habits with you from one job to the next. Little by little, I was starting to do the kind of show I wanted when the axe fell. The station was sold to a company that brokered the time to religious broadcasters, and we were all out of jobs.

I returned to Philadelphia in a state of shock. Here I was on the other side of fifty, asking myself, who am I and what do I want to do with the rest of my life? Did I want to stay in broadcasting, assuming I could get another job? Did I want to expand my counseling agency? Did I want to start a new entrepreneurial venture? Did I want to commit myself to writing as a fulltime career? When I weighed all the possibilities, I realized that I wanted to write more than anything else. Writing was as fundamental to me as breathing—it wasn't a choice; it was something I *had* to do.

Now here comes the tricky part. I knew I wanted to write another book—my sixth—but I didn't know what I wanted to say. Instead of taking the time to reflect upon it, to stand still and commune with myself until some inspiration bubbled up from my subconscious, I began churning out one book proposal after another, mostly revisiting ground I'd already covered. If something I saw in the newspaper or a magazine sparked my interest, I dashed off a book proposal on it, too. All of these proposals were strangely lifeless, lacking the spark of honest feeling, and after getting them rejected once or twice I threw them all out. This was a clear case of letting my reactive impulse to repeat the familiar stymie my creative urge to grow.

Finally, I reached the nadir of futility. I stopped frantically repeating myself or casting about for any topic that caught my fancy, whether I really cared about it or not, and began writing out of the depths of my soul about Rona's accident and how it had changed my life. I felt a conviction about sharing the lessons I'd learned from that experience, and a paraphrase of the Nietzsche quote, "That which does not kill me makes me stronger," popped into my head as the perfect title. Temporarily, I put my ideas on the back burner to collaborate on another book I was asked to write, and when I came back to this book, I knew I had found my voice.

The Truth That Makes Letting Go Easier

The hurt of losing a loved one is much more profound than the pain of getting fired or laid off, but in both instances, grasping this fundamental truth makes letting go easier: *You don't own whatever is given to you in life—it's on loan to you.* Impermanence is a fact of human existence. Nothing in the physical world lasts forever, and any of us can die at any time. Regardless of what life expectancy tables may say, no one is guaranteed any length of years. If we can grasp the concept of living on borrowed time—the transitory, fragile nature of human life—we will not feel so angry or cheated

You don't own whatever is given to you in life—it's on loan to you.

when someone we love dies an early death. We will also be grateful for having this person in our lives for as long as we did. This point was vividly made by a woman whose story is a lesson in the courage both to let go and to endure. It speaks to all those survivors whose loved ones' lives ended too soon.

Edie

Edie Weinstein-Moser, a social worker and ordained interfaith minister, had actual conversations with God in the hospital room where her forty-eight-year-old husband Michael lay dying before a liver transplant could save him. "I called it God wrestling," she says. "I would say, 'He's mine, and you can't have him.' And God would say, 'Uh-uh, he's mine, and he's on loan to you.' That's part of what got me through—to realize that everyone in our lives is simply on loan to us, that maybe forty-eight years is all Michael signed up for, and maybe we did everything we needed to do together and it was time to move on. The love didn't go anywhere. The love is still here. Michael is always going to be a part of my life."

Five years after they were married, Edie and Michael moved from Pennsylvania to Florida to expand their business, a magazine they started and published called *Visions*. Soon after, their home was completely destroyed by Hurricane Andrew. What *wasn't* destroyed sent Edie a message about the endurance of faith. "Nothing in the house was left standing except some spiritual items my parents had given us," she says. "Outside, our six-foot-tall privacy fence surrounding our yard was flattened, but our peace pole—a six-foot obelisk that says, 'May peace prevail on earth' on each of the four sides—was still standing. It was a birthday present for Michael from my parents and me, and we had buried it in a little pot two feet into the ground." Edie and Michael brought the pole back with them when they returned home to Bucks County in Pennsylvania. "Losing our house and almost everything we owned in the hurricane taught me something," Edie says. "Things are not important; people are."

During Michael's six-year-long battle with Hepatitis C, contracted while working as a volunteer on an ambulance squad in the 1970s, Edie became his caretaker. "We all find strengths we never knew we had," she says. "Michael was six feet tall, and I'm five feet, four inches, and I had to help him with feeding, clothing, bathing, lifting him up from the bed or the sofa and walking him around the house with him leaning on me." She practically lived in the intensive care unit in the hospital for the whole five and a half weeks Michael was there and didn't sleep at home in their own bed until the night he died.

As much as their eleven-year marriage was an unusually close and affectionate one, after Michael's death, Edie felt free to create her life in any image that she wanted. "I was still the same person," she says, "but I didn't have to present myself to the world as the same person that I did before. I was sleepwalking through life. I just went with the flow to such an extent that I didn't take responsibility for very much of what I did. As someone whose soul-mate partner—a person I thought I was going to be with for the rest of my life— died, I had to take charge of my life, chart my own course, make all the decisions. I had nobody else to do it for me."

It's not that Edie's role in her marriage held her back in any way. "We had an egalitarian marriage," she says. "In fact, Michael was a lot more domestic than I've ever been. He did the cooking, and he liked to iron. We shared everything—household responsibilities and decisionmaking and childcare of our son Adam, who was eleven when Michael died. So it wasn't the marriage that did it—it was my perception of myself. I was everybody's sweetheart. I didn't want to offend anybody or step on anyone's toes. That doesn't work in business. I wanted to please the advertisers in our magazine so much that I didn't insist they pay us on time, and that was a point of conflict between Michael and me." They sold the magazine six months before Michael died, and Edie is in business for herself now in a way she never was before, "shamelessly self-promoting" her talents as a minister, social worker, speaker, and writer.

As a mother, Edie has changed dramatically, too. "I was a wimp as a mother," she says. "Now I'm the one who's solely responsible for raising Adam, so I need to be firm and directive. That didn't come easily to me, but that was my promise to Michael before he slipped away: I told him I would do everything I could so that our son would grow up to be a good man."

Edie also promised Michael on his deathbed that she would become a minister. "Michael was the one who was going to be a minister," she says. "He enrolled in the New Seminary in New York as a correspondent student because he was too sick to go to class. It was a two-year course, and we couldn't afford for both of us to do it." Edie read to Michael when he couldn't concentrate enough to read, helped him do his homework, and studied along with him. He finished the first year and was prepared to go on to the second when he went into a coma. "On the day he died, I literally heard a voice that said, 'Call the seminary and ask if you can take his place and get ordained instead,'" she says.

When Edie spoke to the dean, she told her they would welcome her into the seminary and let her graduate with Michael's class on two conditions: the first was that she was doing this for herself, not just for Michael; and the second was that she would have to do the first year's work that Michael did all over again and the second year's work, which included papers, tests, oral exams, and two retreats. Edie did it all in record time. "It was a big part of the healing process," she says, "and it gave me a purpose for my life without Michael." Three years since her husband's death, Edie thinks that if Michael were alive today, he would really like who she is as a person more. She says, "I am now the person he always wanted me to be."

A New Picture

When dying is a gradual process, as in Michael's case, acceptance and letting go are easier than for someone whose loved one dies suddenly without any chance to say goodbye. Edie had the advantage of "anticipatory grief"—she knew in a corner of her mind, although she didn't want to accept it at first, that Michael could die. And she also had the time to tell him how much she loved him and make her commitments to him about living her life without him in a way that would honor his memory. That opportunity was sadly denied you if you had coffee with your husband or wife in the morning at the breakfast table and never saw your spouse again, had no trace left of him or her except an urn filled with ashes from a disaster site.

But even when someone is taken from you unexpectedly by a heinous or reckless act, and you have no opportunity say goodbye, the steps you've taken to gain comfort and support will lead you to a time when you are ready for acceptance. The love you had for that person and their love for you will never go away or be altered by time. That connection may be one of the greatest gifts of your life and should never be let go, no matter what new direction you take (you'll find many suggestions for maintaining that connection in Chapter 9). But you might have to let go of some of your old attitudes about how to accept loss—isolating yourself from others, for example—and experience the deep compassion in caring friends and family that will continue to enrich your life. You might also have to let go of some of your old ideas about happiness being contingent on having everything you want and find reasons to enjoy your life, loving the people who are still a big part of it.

As with any of the losses we all experience over a lifetime, acceptance begins with letting go of a picture you had of yourself and going back to the drawing board to create a new one. The old picture was based on ideas you had about what you needed to be, have, or do to find happiness or success, and maybe those ideas were right at that time. Now, with the passage of that old reality—the world you thought would always be—some of those ideas may no longer be right. You need to discard those that are outdated and create a new picture—one that more closely resembles your authentic self, living in the world as you know it now. Clearing away what doesn't fit this new picture will enable you to connect with your creativity, experience your spirituality more fully, and discover a new purpose for living the rest of your life.

Strength-Building Exercise: "What Do You Have to Lose?"

If we take the long view of our lives, we see that at every major juncture of growth there was something we left behind and something new we grasped hold of—in infancy we stopped crawling and learned to walk; in early adolescence we separated from our parents and identified with our peers; in later adolescence we left college and went out into the larger world; as adults we put the single world behind us and entered into marriage. Our spiritual growth follows the same pattern—there are points all along the way when we have to let go of the pillars of our security and take the next step. No growth is accomplished without some loss.

This exercise is designed to make you aware of your growth pattern, the twists and turns it has taken, how at each point of new development, you needed to let go of some internal thing—some perception of yourself, some belief about the world, some attitude toward other people, some all-important goal. Your path to this point has not been in a straight line. All along there were choices you had to make between this course and another; there were events, good as well as bad, that threw you off course and set you in a new direction; there were stumbling blocks in your path that you had to go around; there were uphill battles that made you put yourself into higher gear. I want you to write down all of these past turning points and identify some certainty about your life or some definition of yourself that had to be jettisoned at each juncture so that the journey could continue: Here are some examples of major turning points that can occur in a person's life:

> *Turning Point:*
> > Going away to college:
> *What you had to lose:*
> > Your image of yourself being under
> > your parents' protection.

Turning Point:
> Having to drop out of college
> because of your father's death

What you had to lose:
> Your certainty that your parents
> would always be there for you

Turning Point:
> Marriage

What you had to lose:
> Thinking in terms of "I"
> as you became part of "we"

Turning Point:
> Having to sell your home and
> move to a smaller one

What you had to lose:
> The importance you
> attached to money and status

Turning Point:
> Going back to school

What you had to lose:
> Your belief that you're
> too old to be a student again

Now you must ask, At *this* juncture of my life, what must I let go of, what baggage must I let fall by the wayside so that I can move on and discover a bright new vista opening up before me around the bend in the road? Some sample questions to ask are

- Is the death of someone I love telling me to let go of my image of myself as incomplete without that person?

- Is my illness telling me to let go of my disre-spect for my body? Or to let go of my habit of workaholism or failing to set limits on people who take advantage of me?
- Is the loss of my job telling me to let go of my attitude toward bosses as surrogate parents? Or that I need to let go of my lack of trust in my own instincts or real talents?
- Is my divorce telling me to let go of my pattern of making someone else responsible for my happiness? Or that I need to let go of my belief that I have to control my partner's actions?
- Is my loneliness telling me that I have to let go of my belief that I can't trust anyone and have to keep a safe distance between myself and others?
- Is my trouble with a child telling me to let go of my attitude that I know what's best for him or her? Or that I need to let go of my pattern of self-absorption in my personal goals?

Discern what you need to let go of now, and gather the courage to let go of it. It may take you months, even years, un-til you feel ready to do this, because these patterns, attitudes, and beliefs have become ingrained over time. And remember, a past relationship or situation may not have been wrong for you. It may have been everything you wanted or needed at that time, but your circumstances have changed, and you need to change along with them. You're not renouncing the way you were or what you had; you're opening yourself up to some-thing new. To discover the new, you can't repeat the past. You must let go of it and begin to create a new beginning.

6

Help from the Universe:
External Events Coincide
with Internal Changes

Laurie became a widow at thirty-three when her husband, a firefighter, was killed trying to rescue people from the World Trade Center during the terrorist attacks in 2001. The mother of an infant daughter and a four-year-old son, she felt overwhelmed by the financial crisis facing her—the mortgage, car payments, funeral costs. Laurie didn't like the idea of having to apply to a charitable organization for help, but she put providing for her family above pride. She soon found herself caught up in a bureaucratic maze of application forms and their confusing rules and requirements. Day and night she pored over them and spent hours on the phone talking to representatives of the organizations, sometimes having to repeat the answers to the same questions to three or four different interviewers. Laurie was becoming discouraged and wondered if there wasn't something else she could do to get the financial help she needed right away. "I didn't have anything specific in mind," she says, "but with a six-month-old baby to take care of, I knew it would have to be something I could do at home."

On one of her more frustrating days, Laurie thought she was calling her pediatrician's office to make an appointment for the baby's checkup when she dialed a friend's number by mistake. "I never would have called her during the day because I knew she had a fulltime job," Laurie says, "but I guess I must have been thinking about her." Surprised to hear her friend pick up the phone, Laurie asked, "What are you doing home?" Her friend explained that she had a vacation day coming to her from the insurance company she worked for as a claims adjuster and had taken the time off to attend her daughter's dance recital at school later that day. "I was about to hang up," Laurie says, "when my friend mentioned that she was looking for someone to work at home part-time and type up letters, memoranda, and reports. She said, 'You wouldn't be interested in something like that, would you?'" Laurie jumped at the offer and wound up with a paying job that allowed her to be a stay-at-home mom. "It's enough money to keep a roof over our heads for the time being," she says, "and it's given me the confidence that I can draw on my own resources when I run into a brick wall." What seemed like a mistake that occurred by pure chance—dialing the wrong phone number—turned out to be emotionally meaningful for Laurie as well as financially helpful.

Why Meaningful Coincidences Happen

Nearly everyone has experienced lucky coincidences similar to Laurie's—having some seemingly random incident give us a hand in an extraordinary way when we're struggling to move forward in our lives. In spite of their significance, many of us think of these improbable events only as coincidences instead of seeing them as points of connection between some internal change we're undergoing and the outside world. Our ego doesn't like the idea of an unpremeditated event, one we didn't deliberately cause, having a deep effect on us, so it's easier to chalk such events up to happenstance. But when we surrender our belief in our own omnipotence, we can begin to understand these "synchronicities" as something more. They're the assistance the universe gives us when we let go internally of whatever needs to be relinquished in the interest of spiritual growth. In Laurie's case, as soon as she let go of her total dependence on charitable help and thought about becoming more self-reliant, a synchronistic event gave her a friendly push in that direction.

Synchronicity is a familiar, but perhaps not fully understood, concept to many people. Swiss psychologist Carl G. Jung identified synchronicity as the simultaneous occurrence of an external event that is connected meaningfully, but not by way of cause and effect, with an internal event of emotional significance. In other words, at the point at which a person has shifted gears and is ready to move in a new direction, some mysterious force brings about an outside event that coincides with the person's inner state of readiness. What is that force? Jung gave us the answer to that when he used the word *numinous,* a term he borrowed from theologian Rudolph Otto, to describe the emotional character of a synchronistic event. A numinous experience is an intensely spiritual one, an experience of having gone beyond the limitations of our physical world and come into contact with the Divine. Synchronicity gives us the same feeling of awe and reassurance as surrender—the sense that we are not writing our life stories alone but are co-creating them with a power greater than ourselves. The emotional impact that such an extraordinary event has on us when we're in a transformative state is the force that makes it meaningful. We read the meaning into it, and our interpretation connects our inner state with the outside world in a different way from cause and effect. We didn't plan this event or make it happen, but because it coincides with deep stirrings inside us, we experience it as a moment of connection with the creative energy of the universe.

We are not writing our stories alone but are co-creating them with a power greater than ourselves.

Hooking up synchronistically with exactly the right person at the right moment in time is different from bumping unexpectedly into a long lost friend on the street, chatting with the person for a few moments, and moving on. Synchronistic events don't happen without having a significant influence on you internally at a time when you're undergoing changes in the way you perceive yourself, your life, and the world around you. The letting go of your old pattern opens up a place for the energy of the universe to come in and assist you with a remarkable series of events that help push you forward when you're adrift.

Because a synchronistic event elicits an action from someone else that uncannily fills a need of yours without your having communicated this need to the person beforehand, synchronicity symbolizes the connection that all human beings have with each other. Laurie's friend wasn't aware of her desire to become less dependent on charitable help, and yet when Laurie accidentally dialed her number, her friend, who was home when she normally wasn't, provided her with the means to become less dependent. It was as if her friend, unbidden, somehow sensed what Laurie needed to propel herself toward greater autonomy at the same time that Laurie sensed her friend was looking for help, too. Like the social network of family members and friends and support groups that provide essential comfort and reassurance when you're in a state of emotional upheaval, synchronistic events are a reminder that in this difficult period of transition, you are not alone.

Help from the Universe in Finding Love

During my years of counseling people who thought they would never find love again after the end of a marriage or relationship, I've seen synchronicity bring many of them together with new partners who fit them beautifully. But it doesn't happen until the person has undergone some internal changes, letting go of old ideas, values, and attitudes that are not satisfying any more. Life abounds with stories of single people who stopped frantically searching for a partner and found a new sense of purpose and direction, only to have the "right one" magically pop up in their lives through a chain of unusual events. Some might call this fate, but it was the person's self-acceptance and intent to find joy in his or her own right that enlisted the synchronistic collaboration between the individual and the outside world.

In the first chapter of this book I told you how my disabled daughter, Rona, found love at a convention of a disabilities organization in Nashville when David, her partner for the past seven years, wheeled himself into her life. What I didn't tell you was how synchronicity played a role in this fortuitous event. During the early years of her rehabilitation, Rona defiantly resisted anything that had the word disabled in it. The mental pictures the word evoked were utterly foreign to the image she had of herself as an unimpaired young woman who walked and talked like everyone else. I could understand how she felt. It was impossible for me to say

Rona and disabled in the same breath for a while, and I recoiled when anyone referred to her that way. Like other words with bleak connotations—widow, cancer, terminated—this one took some getting used to. Actually, that's how you know when acceptance has really been accomplished: The words don't stick in your throat any more.

Before she could let go of her old self-concept, Rona clung to the belief that only an able-bodied man would be an appropriate partner for her. It was in this reactive period that she met her first post-accident boyfriend. "Tim" was a thirty-year-old man working his way through college as a part-time desk clerk in the apartment building where Rona lived in a community-based program for brain-injured people. His scholarly bent put him at odds with his hardscrabble working-class family, and his alienation from them made him feel somewhat of an outcast in our society. After years of drifting aimlessly, he was determined to get a higher education and become a history teacher. He met Rona while she was waiting for her stepfather and me to pick her up for our weekly dinner date, and their friendship gradually blossomed into love.

On an intellectual level they were definitely kindred souls. Rona communicated with Tim mostly via messages typed on her computer, and they discovered that they liked the same books, movies, and rock groups, and they began dating. After six months, on Valentine's Day, they became engaged. "I don't think of Rona as disabled," Tim told me, "but as this wonderful person who happens to have disabilities."

They were happy together at first, but then Tim started to show impatience with the everyday complications of living with someone who traveled in a wheelchair. Unintentionally he made Rona feel that she was a burden, and she would often be in tears because of some hurtful thing he'd said or done. Tim also became somewhat overbearing with Rona. He expected her to defer to him, partly because of his beliefs about his role but mainly because of the natural imbalance of power implicit in a relationship between an able-bodied person and one who isn't. There are able-bodied people who don't have this problem, but Tim, for all his good intentions, was uncomfortable with the difficulties he encountered.

Their relationship came to an explosive end when, a week after becoming engaged, Tim decided to go off on a two-week road trip to Graceland without Rona. She pleaded with him to take her, but he was adamant that he needed to be by himself to deal with his father's death the month before. She understood his need to get away, but she could also see a lifetime of sitting home alone, waiting for Tim to come back from wherever he'd gone to "get his head together."

After a tempestuous argument, Tim set off by himself. When he came back, things between them were never the same. Rona realized then that being able-bodied was not an essential part of her vision of a soul mate any more. She'd learned that she wanted someone who not only perceived who she really was but could also identify with her situation and wanted to share his life fully with her as a true partner—someone just like David, the man who came into her life not long after and has been with her ever since.

Rona's breakup with Tim, searingly painful as it was, marked her transition into a more independent woman with a new sense of self and new goals. She moved away from Tim to an apartment in town and took up the banner for the rights of the disabled, no longer ashamed of that part of her identity but embracing it. By letting go of her self-denial, she set the stage for David to make his entrance.

When I tell people who are having trouble with relationships that you have to be ready to find happiness in love, they often say, "I am ready; I've never been more ready in my life." But the desire for something is not the same as readiness for it. Desire is a starting-point, and sometimes it blinds people to the inner work they have to do to get their desires fulfilled. What leftover attitudes or ways of being do they need to let go of that aren't working for them any more? What self-doubts or other limiting thoughts do they have that are holding them back from finding the right person or recognizing who that is? What more do they have to learn about becoming less self-involved and more oriented toward sharing their time, their energy, their assets with others, not just potential partners but anyone who could use their help? When we answer these questions and become sure of our

The desire for something is not the same as readiness for it.

self-worth, sure of our ability to create a satisfying relationship, and sure that we deserve one, we will be in the state of openness and readiness that invites a soul mate to appear.

Help from the Universe in Finding Work

Synchronicity often intervenes on our behalf not only in our love relationships but also in our working lives. Sometimes it comes about when we are so committed to a particular calling that we are willing to suffer daunting rejections, failures, and setbacks, hardening our resolve and learning from our mistakes, until the universe finally gives us an unexpected "break." But synchronicities also occur when we are in the up-in-the-air Reflection Stage, having lost or become frustrated with one job and not certain what we want to do next. If we let go of our fixed ideas of what we can or can't do and open ourselves to whatever opportunities show up, we may find that some random and thoroughly off-the-wall event will answer our prayers in a way we never anticipated. Being open is the key. A closed hand can't accept a gift. Neither can a closed mind. In fact, by being open to all possibilities when we're in transition, we *make* these meaningful coincidences happen out of what might otherwise

> **A closed hand can't accept a gift. Neither can a closed mind.**

have simply been an extraordinary pile-up of events. Hal, a man who came to one of my seminars after he lost his job, reported to me later that he had this very experience.

Ashamed of losing his longtime job as a bank officer, Hal continued to take the train to and from his workplace for months after he was laid off, pretending he was still going to his office. "Intellectually, I knew I wasn't to blame for getting caught in a downsizing," he says, "but I still felt worthless. I didn't want anyone to know I was out of work, so I acted like a fugitive on the lam." The truth is, Hal was running away from himself.

When he forced himself to start looking for a job, the headhunters he saw didn't paint a very rosy picture. "They told me there was a glut on the job market for unemployed managers in their mid-fifties." The newspaper leads Hal followed up were no more encouraging. "The human resources people used clever buzzwords like *over-qualified*," he says, "but I could see that I was a victim of age discrimination— and there wasn't a thing I could do about it."

Hal became increasingly depressed and withdrawn, fearful that he would never find work again. His wife became alarmed when their savings began to evaporate, and she prevailed upon him to go to their local unemployment office.

"For me, that was like an alcoholic's hitting bottom," Hal says. "I stood in that line and thought to myself, 'So this is what your life has come to. What a loser you are.' Then I started getting mad. I was angry at a system that discarded loyal employees, people who worked their tails off, like so many pieces of trash."

It was at this point that Hal came to my seminar. He was encouraged to let go of his illusions about the nature of the working world and his attitude toward himself as a loser and to use his anger to ignite his energy and imagination. That was a breakthrough for Hal. "I stopped feeling sorry for myself, even stopped feeling angry at the system, and became more determined than ever to find work," he remembers. "I wanted to work not just for the money, although God knows that was important, but to be productive in my own way, use the skills that I had, regardless of the status of the job or what it paid." Once he began to think of himself as more than the job that had defined him and was open to whatever life might present, his confidence returned. He says, "I knew there was something out there for me—I could almost hear it calling my name—and I felt that if I kept banging on doors, one would open."

Two weeks later, Hal was sitting in a snack bar at the airport, waiting for his wife's plane to arrive from Cleveland. She was returning from a visit to her elderly parents who lived there, and the plane was late. A man carrying a sandwich tray passed Hal's table, then came back and asked in surprise, "Hal, is that you?" It was Josh, an old college classmate who used to work with Hal at the same bank years ago before he took a job somewhere else. Hal and Josh had enjoyed each other's company outside of work, played racquetball together, and were both active in political campaigns for the same candidates. Josh was also having a quick bite while waiting for the plane from Cleveland to arrive with some business contacts of his, and Hal invited him to join him at his table.

Josh told Hal that leaving the bank was the best thing he'd ever done. He went to work raising money for the endowment fund of the university where he and Hal first met and was now director of the endowment department, soliciting contributions from contributors around the country and the world. This was not the kind of position Hal had ever sought, but to his surprise he found himself asking Josh if he could join his staff. "I expected him to turn me down flat," Hal says, "but he seemed happy to hire me. We always liked each other, but more than that, I think he admired my guts—at my age, I was willing to try something I'd never done before and didn't care what it paid. He saw that what was all-important to me was putting my financial knowledge and skills to good use in something that mattered to me."

This was certainly a meaningful coincidence—a delayed airplane flight bringing a compatible, empathic former colleague into Hal's life at a time when he was in need of a new beginning and open to one. The random reappearance of an old friend when we feel isolated and troubled is the universe's way of reminding us that our connections to people, formed with affection and shared interests, are there all the time, even when the people have dropped out of sight. "It never would have occurred to me to call Josh up and ask him for a job even if I knew where he was," Hal says, "so I have to think that some kind of divine intervention had a hand in bringing us together. That meeting changed my life. In the banking industry I was helping people save their money or invest it for personal gain, and now I'm showing them how to do something with it that is really valuable on a larger scale."

Synchronicity shows us that help from the universe is always available to us when we let go of a way of thinking or being that limits us and form the intent to expand ourselves. Had Hal not been open to taking on a new challenge at a pay cut, the chance meeting still would have happened and been pleasant, but it would not have ended in employment. When we move in the direction of becoming more of who we are, our new sense of purpose invites forces much larger and more powerful than ourselves to bring into our lives events that we recognize and seize upon as fortuitous synchronicities.

Making Miracles Happen: Nonspecific Intent

The confusion and uncertainty you feel when your life is up in the air make you want to find solutions to your problem right now. You want the universe to intervene immediately with some miraculous event that will answer your prayers— bring you a job, a soul mate, a cure for your illness. But remember, it's our *openness*, our inner state of readiness to receive help, that sends it our way. For those of us who pray, prayer works best when we think of ourselves as co-creators with God, not bosses who give God a to-do list and expect it to get checked off. When we let go of asking for specific outcomes by a specific time in a specific manner and focus on becoming what we're each individually meant to be—the contributions we're supposed to make with our special gifts in however many years of life we're given—the answers will come. The answer may be different from what we want in the short term, but it will always be what we need for the long-term realization of our strengths.

When you ask for help in any area of your life—healing your emotional pain or loneliness, bringing you financial security, curing an illness— take your personal agenda out of it. Don't ask for some specific thing you

Focus on how you want to be, not what you want to have.

want the world to give you, or you may be very disappointed with what you get. Instead, focus on the kind of human being you want to be—how you want to be, not what you want to have—and ask the world to help you become that person. Remember, your circumstances don't define you, so concentrate on the personal qualities you want to exemplify rather than on what you want to acquire.

Connect with the field of *all* possibilities without narrowing the choices down to the one or two you're capable of perceiving with your limited human means. Let go of anticipating what you think you need, and be ready to accept what is spiritually best for you. Ask for what you want, not for your own gratification but for the purpose of becoming truer to who you are and bringing fulfillment to others. Instead of asking for this company to hire you or this person to marry you, for example, put out a clear intention with all your heart, mind, soul, and power to become a more productive or loving person, and see what happens. When you're motivated by that kind of unselfish, nonspecific intent, coupled with passion and conviction, you get results. You'll experience yourself in the right place at the right time to meet the person you need to meet, often in a way beyond anything you could have imagined.

As co-creators of our lives, we can enlist outside help, but we still have to do the hard inner work ourselves. Synchronicities are miracles in the sense that they go beyond the normal way life operates, and in order to make them happen, we have to go beyond our normal way of being, too. If we resist sinking into depression and bitterness after a devastating loss and react instead with trust in ourselves to grow stronger from it, we have put ourselves in a position for some meaningful coincidence to change the course of our lives. Rona's meeting David and Hal's meeting Josh occurred when they had both come to terms with what they lost and sailed back into the world, determined to find a new place for themselves in it.

Meaningful coincidences happen in more subtle ways, too. Connie was lost in grief when her son was killed by a drunk driver. Her friends were compassionate and supportive, but they couldn't pull her out of her depression. Finally, Connie reached a point where she knew that as much as she hated what happened to her son, she would have to learn to live with the loss. Unable to fall asleep, she was watching television late one night when she came across an old movie she'd seen before, but she decided to watch it again. It was *Ordinary People*, the story of a young man whose guilt at surviving his younger brother's tragic death in a boating accident drives him to attempt suicide, something his emotionally remote mother can't handle. Suddenly Connie realized how her own grief and anger were making her younger son feel guilty that he was still alive. That chance stumbling upon the movie motivated her to draw upon her strength and become a more loving mother to her surviving son and to make the love and support of her friends and family a source of happiness in her life.

The Principle of Unconditional Happiness

Appreciating the things we do have instead of focusing on what we've lost is the kind of positive internal change that promotes healing and attracts into our lives more things to be grateful for. Yes, the pain we feel from a loss takes a long time to go away and never disappears entirely, but we need to decide that we can still be happy—unconditionally happy—in spite of the calamity. When I speak of "unconditional happiness," I mean that, like unconditional love, it's not predicated on certain conditions or requirements being met. If someone we love disappoints us or makes us angry temporarily, we still love the person anyway. We don't cut off our love for the time being and wait to restore it until the person has done something to please us again. The capacity to feel happiness must also not be conditional on having everything exactly as we want it. To postpone happiness until some vague time in the future is to make the present meaningless. Deciding to be happy right now, for no other reason than we *can* be happy in the face of adversity, gives us the strength to live on.

Ross, a former client at my counseling agency, is an example of what I mean. At thirty-one, married and the father of

> **Happiness must not be conditional on having everything exactly as we want it.**

two young children, Ross lost his eyesight as a result of complications stemming from juvenile diabetes. His vision was gone but not his capacity to enjoy life in spite of his loss. He could have said, "I'll be happy only when I can see again," but he was not content to wait until some miracle restored his sight. Nor did he feel that his life was over because his career as an engineer had ended. Instead, inspired by the therapy he received in the initial adjustment phase after he lost his sight, he entered a master's program in psychology, planning to become a therapist himself. Although he can't see a majestic sunset or the faces of his loved ones any more, by filling his mind with learning and delighting in the discovery of a new dimension of himself, he has found a way to be unconditionally happy.

When we choose to appreciate the sources of happiness the gift of life has given us rather than dwell on what we lack, the universe joins with us to help us stand up after we fall. The enormous outpouring of love and compassion and financial aid for survivors of loved ones killed in the terrorist attacks, much of it coming from strangers, is an example of how the universe sends help to those who have the spirit to carry on after the cruelest of blows.

A corollary to the principle of unconditional happiness is that it's our effort to resist unhappiness and transform it into positive action that brings us new opportunities for fulfillment. We have to *earn* the miracles we wish for by striving to find the strength within ourselves to be resilient and grow spiritually. When we ask whatever larger-than-life power we believe in to do this or do that to make our problems go away, we're not showing any willingness on our part to live with our problems and co-create solutions that will enrich our lives. Our connection with the spiritual world is all about our own pain and not about seeking support for our growth. We're too focused on end results and not enough on the process. But if we focus on finding greater inner strength so that the demolition of our certainties doesn't shatter us but instead helps further our development, the specifics will take care of themselves in ways beyond our imagining.

Strength-Building Exercise:
"How Do You Want to Be?"

In this period of transition, you can receive help from the universe in the form of extraordinary outside events that coincide with your inner state of readiness to move ahead and become truer to who you really are. These meaningful coincidences, or synchronicities, are always preceded by an internal letting go of some of your previous attitudes, beliefs, or goals in response to the misfortune you've suffered. If you focus on becoming the kind of person you want to be in the world, what you want to contribute rather than on what you want to have happen—getting a job, finding a new partner—synchronistic events will come your way.

Formulate an intent that reflects the internal changes you are experiencing—how you are redefining yourself or what attitudes or values you are letting go of in response to your adversity. Write a brief sentence summarizing your new outlook. Instead of wishing for specifics to happen, strive to become the kind of person you want to be. Here are some examples:

- Instead of *please make me get this job*, ask, *please help me find satisfaction in work and contribute something of value, whether it's in this job or another.*
- Instead of *please make this person the right one for me*, ask, *please help me to be a loving, supportive, self-respecting partner in a committed relationship, whether it's with this person or someone else.*
- Instead of *please help my child walk again*, ask, *please help me love my child unconditionally, whether he recovers fully or not.*
- Instead of *please make this sickness go away*, ask, *please give me the strength to take charge of my health and bear whatever I have to bear with courage and grace.*

- Instead of *please let me win this battle* (whatever the battle may be), ask, *please give me the wisdom and determination to grow emotionally, mentally, and spiritually from this situation and recreate my life.*

When you intend to move in accordance with your own deepest motivations—to move *with* what and who you are, not against—you are moving in harmony with the universal life force. Your intention may bring what is hoped for or something different, but it *will* be rewarded.

Part III

Rebuilding

7

Seeing Loss as Possibility

On November 11, 2001, exactly two months after the World Trade Center attacks, the *New York Times Magazine* came out with a special issue devoted entirely to "Beginnings." The whole thrust of the issue was the need to turn from mourning New York's losses to the positive work of rebuilding the city and making it an even better city than it was before the attacks. There were suggestions for what to do with the Ground Zero site, ranging from building an entirely new complex with space for a memorial to extending Battery Park City into the site and making the whole area one big, happy city. Regardless of the particular plans, the message of the magazine was clear: It was time to emerge from the shadows of grief and see, in the acres of scorched rubble where the Trade Center once stood, the possibilities of what the city could become. New Yorkers had already exhibited the courage, compassion, generosity, determination, and spirit of resilience that made them admired around the world. Rebuilding the city—not just reconstructing what they had but creating a city of the future—would benefit them emotionally as a way of channeling their grief, socially as a way of bringing the community together, and spiritually as a life-affirming response to the heinous evil they had encountered.

The New York experience is a paradigm of what each of us has to go through when we're dealing with our own tragedies and losses. First there is the overwhelming grief in the Rupture Stage—some calamity has reduced part of your life to Ground Zero—that blinds you to everything except your own pain. Then there is the period of uncertainty in the Reflection Stage when you are letting go of what was and opening yourself up to something new. And now there is the Rebuilding Stage when you begin to see in the empty space left by your loss different possibilities for creating a new reality that has its own compelling attractions.

Using Creativity to Survive Change

The task of this stage is to reframe loss as possibility. This is the time when your creativity comes into play. Because we're so used to thinking of creativity as a personal trait, it's easy to miss the fact that the greatest spur to it often comes from changes outside ourselves. Terrible as these changes might be, they force us to do what we would not do willingly: We do what the soul is all about and take the next step up the winding spiral staircase of our spiritual growth. Helpless as we may feel, we have a secret weapon at our command. We've been provided with creativity—the ability to see things in a new light—as the means to deal with the losses that our spiritual evolution demands.

Creativity is wired into all of us—not just writers, musicians, artists, inventors, or others we normally think of as creative—as a survival mechanism for confronting sudden dangers and taking advantage of the opportunities that arise in the unexpected. Another inborn force, called entropy, motivates us to conserve our strength and get by with the least effort. Entropy is a more primitive and powerful force than creativity, and it makes us fear and resist change. Most of us would rather snuggle into some comfort zone and stay there rather than wrestle with the loss of the familiar. All our lives we are whipsawed by these two opposite imperatives programmed into the brain—creativity pushing us to move forward, entropy pulling us to stay put. We can't let entropy win. If we do, our lives will be frozen at the point of the unexpected loss, and we'll be stuck in time, constantly reliving the past, never able to move forward and discover joy again. On the grander scale of life, if entropy wins, what will happen to the human race? With no discovery of new ways of thinking and doing, our evolution will end, and we will descend into chaos.

Matthew's story is an example of how the creative process works when adversity shatters the landscape of our lives and we have to pick up the pieces and fashion them into something new. His was not the loss of a loved one, but it created a devastating hole in his world nonetheless.

Matthew

At forty-two, Matthew was in the prime of his career as a busy obstetrician-gynecologist when life as he knew it came apart. He lost his right hand in a skiing accident and, as a result, would never be able to practice medicine again. "My whole future was smashed like my hand in a crash on a ski slope," Matthew says. "For me, losing my hand was a metaphor for losing my purpose in life. Being a physician was in my genes. My mother and father were both doctors, and there was never any question that I'd be one, too. I couldn't see anything ahead of me."

The worst moment came when Matthew went back to his office for the last time before another doctor would be taking over his practice. "I looked at all the pictures on the wall of happy couples with their newborn babies I'd helped bring into the world," Matthew says, "and I burst into tears. I sat at my desk, crying like a baby myself, for what seemed like hours."

Then another catastrophe hit. Matthew's wife was diagnosed with uterine cancer and had to undergo surgery, chemotherapy, and radiation treatments. "We felt that all our luck had run out," he says. "We just wanted to withdraw from life, but we had to keep fighting off defeatism for the sake of our three children who were still in school." Matthew thought of leaving medicine entirely and going into another field, but there was nothing that appealed to him or that he felt equipped to do. "Anything I was even mildly interested in, like forensic law, would take years of study," he says, "and I didn't feel I could take on learning a whole new profession with my wife being ill. Her prognosis was good because they caught the cancer early, but I wanted to be there for her when she needed me."

People told Matthew about career opportunities, and he researched them in books, magazines, and on the Internet; but nothing called out to him the way medicine did. "You just can't do something for the sake of doing it," he says. "There has to be desire."

After his wife finished chemotherapy and was feeling better, Matthew took her for a brief vacation in the Bahamas. "We were walking on the beach, drinking in the incredible beauty around us," he says, "and I was thinking what a miracle nature is, the way I did every time I delivered a baby. All of a sudden it hit me. There was no way I would leave medicine. If I couldn't practice it, I would teach it. Maybe that was what I was meant to do all along."

Once Matthew saw in his loss the possibility of continuing to satisfy his deepest desires in work in a different way, synchronicity came to his aid with a chance meeting at exactly the right time to help him move on. He was coming out of a drugstore when he bumped into a former professor of his who still remembered what an outstanding student Matthew was and was sorry to hear about his accident. Two weeks later the professor called with the news that there was an opening for an associate professor in the ob-gyn. department and asked if Matthew would be interested in the position. "I was flabbergasted," he says. "It was the answer to my prayers, and I accepted on the spot." As soon as he hung up the phone, Matthew began thinking about the kind of teacher he would be. What approach would he take? How would he connect with his students? What would make him a good teacher? "I played the whole thing over in my mind again and again, elaborating on it, and by the time the semester started, I was ready."

Today Matthew is finding as much, if not more, fulfillment teaching his craft to medical students as he had delivering babies. "When I see a class of my students graduate and go out into the field as new doctors," he says, "I feel the same old thrill I used to feel when I watched a new baby being born. It's very gratifying to know you're making a contribution to the profession you love in any way that you can make it."

The Five Steps to a Creative Solution

Every life situation offers you the opportunity to be creative, to be open to answers that move you toward a new purpose consistent with your deepest self and gratifying actions that serve others as well as yourself. Keeping the big picture in mind—the certainty that whatever you are experiencing will contribute to your development into a more fulfilled and empowered human being—will help you find answers to the practical questions that have to be resolved. Each adversity brings its own particular problems: financial matters, medical treatment issues, raising a family with only one parent, finding suitable work. Some solutions may come quickly, but others take you through the same struggle that Matthew experienced until he accessed his creativity and discovered a new purpose in life with its own richness and rewards.

How did Matthew do it? The sudden "aha!" moment he had on the beach in the Bahamas didn't just fall like a coconut from a palm tree. He prepared his mind for the insight—that he should become a teacher of the specialty he once practiced—by immersing himself in the problem of losing his career and considering the possibility of going into another field. Then he gathered information about other occupations and let his thoughts about them incubate for a while. When he couldn't stand to think about his dilemma any more, he took a break, and *boom!*—that's when his epiphany hit him. Teaching medicine, when he evaluated it against the other types of work he'd weeded out for one reason or another, was the answer he'd been searching for. Then came the offer from his former professor. After Matthew accepted the offer, he went over his decision to be a teacher and elaborated on it, turning it this way and that, refining his plans, until he was ready to translate his choice into a reality.

The creative process has been traditionally described as taking the five steps that Matthew went through:

- Preparation—immersion in the problem
- Incubation—churning ideas around unconsciously

- Insight—suddenly seeing how the pieces of the puzzle fall together
- Evaluation—deciding whether the insight is worth pursuing
- Elaboration—translating the decision into a reality

We don't take these steps in a linear fashion but instead double back on them, go through loops, and have flashes of separate insights that can take a while to jell into a single, coherent idea. It's important to know how this process works so you don't feel stupid or berate yourself for being indecisive when you begin to see all the possibilities that are out there in the wake of a personal disaster. You're confused, not because there isn't an answer but only because there are so many questions. Should I go back to school or get a job, stay here or move away, look for attendant care or find a facility, get surgery or try alternative treatment, borrow money or sell the house? and on and on. Freedom of choice can stir up enormous anxiety, mainly because of our culture's "quick fix" mentality. Panic-stricken because you can't hit on a solution quickly, you may jump on the mental treadmill of rumination or run out and settle for the first option that crosses your line of vision. Either of these two—rumination or rashness—will abort the unfolding of the creative process that leads to genuine insights.

Your life is a creative work in progress. Sometimes it flows freely, but there are other times when it requires a topsy-turvy period of turning this way and that, considering ideas and discarding them. As you are writing the story of your life, bear in mind that authors typically discard more than they keep. Jonathan Franzen, for example, who won the National Book Award in 2001 for his bestseller

Corrections, a novel about relations between parents and children in a dysfunctional family, threw out *thousands* of pages during the writing of the book. Likewise, when you're creating your life, you need to exhibit the same willingness to let your goals and deepest feelings guide you toward what is essentially right for you and discard what isn't. Keep your mind open to the possibilities, and be flexible but determined to make choices that will push the envelope of your growth.

Logical analysis is valuable in the earlier stages of the creative process, when you're lining up your options, and later when you're implementing your choices. But ordinary reasoning is often a major obstacle to discovering new life-changing possibilities. Often that flash of insight occurs when, like Matthew, you *stop* thinking about what to do and divert your mind in some pleasant or absorbing activity or visit a setting where you feel close to nature. You have to suspend logical thinking before new insights will come. Their birth occurs when you shut off your conscious mind and are most in touch, through your unconscious, with the creative energy of the universe. Unhampered by the limitations of ordinary logic, your unconscious can organize and reorganize information rapidly, move experiences around and combine them in remarkable ways, and give you a whole new outlook on some aspect of yourself or your external reality. Diversion—not running away, but letting your mind rest—lets your creativity's unseen hand switch on that famous light bulb in your head. Give enlightenment a chance to happen. Stand still, and let what is special within you show you the way.

Stand still, and let what is special within you show you the way.

Choices from the Heart

Unlike decisions that can be made on a factual basis by collecting information, weighing the pros and cons, and arriving at a clear-cut answer, such as deciding to rent an apartment rather than buy a home, creative solutions are choices from the heart. Insight is more than a simple flash of an answer to your problem; it involves an important change in perspective, an awareness of some significant aspect of yourself that you hadn't been aware of before. To gain insight is to let go of your old take on things in favor of a new and more productive way of looking at yourself or at someone else or at some facet of external reality. Not only do you see your situation with a fresh pair of eyes but you also experience yourself differently, and because of your new perspective, you create a fundamentally different state of mind. This "thinking outside of the box," as it's commonly called, gives you a clearer picture of who you are as opposed to what others might think of you.

Ginny

Ginny, a thirty-eight-year-old graduate student, suffered years of unhappiness before she gained insights into herself that liberated her from the self-imposed prison her life had become. "To the outside world, I was the picture of success," Ginny says. "I was married to the same man for fourteen years, had two healthy young children, was making good money as a paralegal for a large law firm, was an officer of the PTA at my children's school, and had many wonderful friends. Everyone who knew me thought I was a happy woman leading a busy, full life." But that was only one side of the story. The other side, hidden from public view, was that Ginny had been severely depressed and anxious for almost two years, ever since her mother's death. She was taking medication, but even that didn't seem to help. There were days when she could barely drag herself out of bed in the morning to go to work, and when she got there, she functioned like a robot on remote control.

"I'd been hiding my pain for many years," Ginny says, "and I think losing my mother was the last straw. She was my best friend in the whole world. My father was very remote and critical, always finding fault with me, and I married the same kind of unloving, emotionally abusive man. My husband had a violent temper with me but was very charming when other people were around, so nobody knew what my life with him was like when we were alone."

Ginny was on the verge of an emotional breakdown when she was called into the conference room at work one day and told she was being laid off for economic reasons. "I should have been devastated," Ginny says, "but all I felt was a flood of relief. I was overworked and underappreciated in my job, the same way I was in my marriage. I felt demeaned all the time, but I just put on a mask and pretended to myself and everyone else that everything was okay."

Her husband's complete lack of sympathy when he learned Ginny lost her job was like a lightning rod for her discontent. "He made me feel it was my incompetence that cost me my job, not the economy. His arrogance was unbelievable. It made me think, 'Why have I stayed with this man all these years?' Something broke inside me, and I became enraged. We had a screaming fight, and I ran out of the house in tears, got into my car and drove for hours, trying to calm myself down. By the time I got home, I knew things had to change."

In the ensuing weeks, rather than rushing out to find another job, Ginny spent time at home by herself and tried to figure out why things had gone so wrong in her life and where she wanted to go from there. And she acquired some powerful insights. "Suddenly I saw that the beliefs I had about myself were the cause of all my troubles," Ginny says. "Other people—my husband, my bosses—were only mirroring those beliefs. That didn't excuse their behavior, but it made it understandable. They were as deceived about me as I was deceived about myself. The image I fought so hard to protect all those years wasn't me. I felt that a heavy fog had suddenly lifted, and I was seeing myself and the world as it really was for the first time."

Her desire to present herself to the world as a more authentic person—to give her soul a voice—opened the door to possibilities that Ginny never would have considered before. For months, a back-and-forth dialogue played in her head. She was in a quandary, asking herself the same questions— "Should I get a divorce?" and "Should I get another paralegal job or try something else?"—without being able to answer them. Then Ginny started using new words to frame her questions, restating them in a different way. Instead of asking, "Should I get a divorce?" she asked, "What have I thought a marriage should be? Are my expectations the same now, or have they changed? Can this marriage meet my expectations, or do I need to be on my own?" Instead of asking whether she should look for another paralegal job or try something else, she asked, "Does the field I've been in appeal to my basic interests? Does the work use my abilities to the fullest extent? How important is the amount of money I earn? How do I want to spend my time each day, doing what kinds of work, finding what kinds of rewards, being in what kind of environment, associating with what kinds of people?"

Ginny discovered that asking questions that put her needs, goals, desires, and values at the center of the choice stimulated her creative thinking about her problems and was

Put who you are at the center of a choice, and the answers will start to come.

the first step toward resolving them. As long as she asked in an abstract manner what was the right or wrong thing to do, her problems defied resolution. But as soon as she made who she was and what she wanted to do with her life the focal point of her choice, the answers began to come. Ginny decided to get a divorce. Her husband refused to accept any responsibility for improving the relationship, and she felt it would be best to end a marriage lacking in love and respect. Having let go of her old limiting beliefs about herself, she also decided not to get another job as a paralegal but to become a lawyer. She was drawn to the field of law and wanted to stay in it at a level that would stretch her untapped abilities and bring her deeper satisfactions.

Although she knew it was going to be hard to put herself through law school as a single mother, Ginny's commitment to the possibility of a new life fired up her motivation to do whatever it took to implement her choice. Even so, juggling her studies with working part-time as a paralegal and tending to her children's needs was more grueling than she anticipated. She spent many nights studying until three in the morning. "There were times when I felt overwhelmed and was tempted to quit," she says, "but it's amazing what you can do when you're following your heart." With two semesters left to graduation and the light at the end of the tunnel almost visible, she says, "I didn't change my life—I saved it."

Choosing Life

People like Ginny are motivated to save themselves by their own internal dissatisfaction with their current way of being, and others are pushed to do it by an outside event, but in either case the choice is clear: Either choose entropy, which is a kind of death, or choose creativity and an authentic life. The choice can be particularly agonizing for people who were leading a normal life one day and, like Matthew, woke up the next day disabled. Before Rona's accident, I had no inkling of the awe-inspiring creativity of the many people who have escaped imprisonment by damaged bodies and discovered possibilities for contribution equal to anything made by the unimpaired. Their stories seem to have a common thread. They went from not being sure if they wanted to live or die to consciously, and with determination, choosing life—not just sitting around at home feeling sorry for themselves and collecting their disability checks once a month—but *living*.

Once they committed themselves to that choice, these people who thought they had no future began to see possibilities for continuing their growth and making worthwhile contributions even if they couldn't go back to what they were before. A talented dancer, who lost her leg in an accident, found the right prosthesis and is still dancing professionally. A business owner and family man, who never finished high school before he became a paraplegic, used his computer to help him earn his GED at forty and is now getting a college degree in counseling. A sales representative, who lost his sight and his job at the same time, parlayed his sense of humor and talent for mimicry into a comedy routine and is performing regularly.

Seven and a half million disabled people, many of them wheelchair bound, are in the workplace, participating in company meetings through the Internet and using assistive technologies to overcome their disabilities. These people, and countless others like them, famous and unknown, have employed their creativity to surmount staggering hardships and discover possibilities for fulfillment in their losses. They testify to the elemental truth that the most important answer to loss is to continue to live.

The most important answer to loss is to continue to live.

Making Possibilities Visible

Necessary as it is to share your emotions and thoughts with others when you're experiencing the immediate effects of a raw adversity, as you gain distance from it, you need to schedule regular periods of solitude. You can't hear the murmurings of your inner voice when other voices around you are crowding it out. Carving out some time to be alone with your thoughts for a little while every day, as Ginny did when she sat home after the family left in the morning, gives you a chance to commune with yourself. Find the time to jog, take a walk, sit quietly by yourself early in the morning or after dinner at night, or go on a weekend retreat in a tranquil setting away from the noise and confusion of urban life. During this private time, focus on what your deepest inclinations are—what you enjoy, what inspires you, what is closest to your heart—apart from others' judgments or expectations of you or your old perceptions of yourself. As you question what you really want to do with your life, the possibilities will begin to present themselves.

Keeping a journal or a daily log can help you organize your thoughts and process them. Seeing the contents of your mind in black and white on a sheet of a paper is illuminating. The journal should be an honest recording of your subjective thoughts and feelings about the issues confronting you, your interactions with other people, or the decisions you're trying to make rather than a simple account of your external day-to-day experiences. Try to write each page in a stream-of-consciousness fashion, almost like automatic writing, letting your emotions, concerns, ideas, and desires pour out without inhibition. I've kept such a journal myself during difficult times, and when I look back on it now I see how doing so helped me get a handle on my confusion and uncertainty. The short time I spent each day writing down the thoughts that came into my head helped me winnow out possibilities I felt were not right for me until the ones that were right began to take shape.

Shifting your attention away from your loss and refocusing it on emerging possibilities is immensely reassuring. You can see, maybe for the first time, that your life is only temporarily stalled and will move forward again when you narrow the possibilities down and commit to a choice from the heart.

Strength-Building Exercise: "What Are the Possibilities?"

This exercise will help you reframe loss as possibility and get a sense of control over your situation. The first part of this exercise will help you recognize and appreciate what has *not* been lost. Make a list of the twenty most important things you still have in your life: the love of family members, health, intelligence, friends, a home, work, skills, financial savings, sight, hearing, speech, mobility, music, art, books, movies, access to information, community resources, etc. Take stock of all that you have, and be grateful for it.

For the second part of this exercise, make a list of every possible solution to your situation you can think of. These are some sample questions to help you conjure up the possibilities:

- What has given me the most pleasure in my life?
- What am I free to do now that I couldn't before?
- What do I value most—family, social contact, intimacy, physical activity, wealth, idealism, knowledge, self-expression, personal achievement?
- What do (or did) I like about my work? What don't I like about it? If I had it to do over again, what would I be doing?
- What do I find most satisfying in a relationship?
- What kind of people do I like to be around?
- What do I like about the area where I live? What don't I like about it? Is there another area I might like more?
- What people do I consider role models?

After you've drawn up a list of possibilities, gather information on each one from various resources—the Internet, books and magazine articles, organizations, knowledgeable personal contacts. Consider the pros and cons of each possibility, be realistic about the feasibility of each, but bear in mind that your own feelings and goals are paramount.

8

Creating a New Dream

We've seen how acceptance of a misfortune means letting go of who you were and what you thought your world would always be in order to create a new reality. The most important hidden blessing in adversity is that it makes you question what life is all about, and that questioning leads you to discover who you are, why you are on this earth, and how you can make your life matter.

When an outside event shatters your world, it makes you break through to yourself in new ways. If you haven't done the hard work of being true to yourself, a crisis blows away the static that has kept you from hearing the call of your soul. The static is all the illusions you have about who you are or what your true purpose in life is—pseudo certainties that have not come to you from the depths of your own unique being but are messages you've picked up from your parents, the culture, religious doctrines, peer pressure, your defenses against emotional pain, or your fears. The misfortune that shakes your soul clears away the "soul static" and lets you connect with your truest, one-of-a-kind self and the particular destiny that only you were born to fulfill. Even if you have already been living purposefully and experiencing unconditional happiness, after a crisis has disrupted your intact world, you need to reassess how you want to live your life *now.* You need to delve deep within yourself, connect with that core of your identity again and let it guide you toward making a new beginning.

When an outside event shatters your world, it makes you break through to yourself in new ways.

This discernment of the deepest level of yourself applies to your own personal growth and your relations with others as well as your ambitions, vocation, or career. Your mission in life may not be a contribution in the public arena but in the development of your inner strength and some new dimension within yourself. If you've lost a loved one, for example, it may very well be that transforming anger and sadness into compassion and generosity toward others, thereby learning how to become responsible for your own unconditional happiness, is your one true purpose in the world.

How do you know what your one true purpose is, and how can you tell which of the possibilities you've uncovered at this point in the Rebuilding Stage fits that purpose? You must review your list carefully, narrow it down, and pick the one possibility that resonates with the unique human quality you personify after a crisis or tragedy—your perspective on life, your basic nature, your talent, your skills, your knowledge, your wisdom. Ask yourself what you now want to say to the world in your own voice and which possibility best accommodates your message. A forfeited old dream of yours might seem unrealistic now—I'm too old, I don't have enough money, I'm inexperienced—but if the dream still fills you with that same passion and intuitive feeling of rightness for you, don't give up on it. The strength of your conviction can help you change your perception of yourself and motivate you to answer the call of your soul that you may have lacked the resolve or opportunity to answer before.

Following Your Pattern

Some of us have a sudden epiphany about our one true purpose in life and it never wavers, while for many others, the direction is not so clear. If you're one of the latter, you may have taken one path, then switched to another, and are now back at a crossroads again. But for all your fits and starts, you can find clues to a pattern that leads you in the direction of your primary mission in life. The clues are recurring ideas, fantasies, images, memories, impressions, longings, or dreams that signify the road your soul wants you to travel to reach the heights of your own unique reality. A movie scene that drew you into it and made you wish you were there, a conversation that sticks in your mind, some childhood activity you loved that you've always wanted to repeat, a yearning you've had for a long time, some work you imagine yourself doing, a dream that recurs again and again—these can all be part of a pattern guiding you toward the one possibility your soul is calling out for you to pursue.

Very often, your pattern involves something you've always had an affinity for but never thought of doing professionally until some outside event propels you into it. And when it does, the hidden blessings can be all the more meaningful because of the searching and struggle you had to go through to find them.

Rose

Rose's story illustrates how a hankering of ours can lead us down one path, then another, and finally into our true calling when an unexpected misfortune creates a need for us to take still another new direction. A former nun who entered the convent right after high school, Rose came from a large Irish Catholic family and always loved babies. She taught children in the convent, but that didn't satisfy her yearning to have children of her own, so she left the convent after six years and got married.

After her first child was born and she was having trouble getting pregnant again, Rose and her husband adopted a baby girl given birth to by an alcoholic mother incapable of taking care of her. The baby, who weighed less than three pounds at birth but otherwise seemed normal, started showing signs of neurological damage and mental retardation early on. When she was eighteen months old, she was diagnosed with Fetal Alcohol Syndrome. Her uncontrollable hyperactivity was a constant source of worry for Rose and created one hair-raising crisis after another for the family. Rose's husband worked a night shift from 2:00 PM until 10:00 PM and wasn't around to help. At one point, Rose's older daughter asked her, "Why are you keeping this baby?" And Rose answered, "I wouldn't send you back if I thought something was wrong with you. Why would I send her back?"

Besides arousing her maternal instinct, the baby's condition stirred another profound sense of purpose in Rose. "From my Catholicism and working-class background, I was the kind of person who always stood up for the underdog," she says. "I was a teacher, but I really wanted to be a social worker. I grew up in an alcoholic, abusive household, and I think in a way I wanted to rescue this baby, and I was rescuing myself at the same time." Rose credits Alma, her adopted child, for pushing her to act on her "rescuer" fantasy and her social worker and champion-of-the-underdog sensibilities. It was the difficulty of finding services for Alma when it became too dangerous to keep her at home that pushed Rose to go back to school and become an advocate for children instead of a teacher of them. While she was still raising Alma and her other daughter at home, Rose went into therapy and was encouraged to go back to college at thirty-seven to earn her undergraduate degree. "When I got back into school, I realized that I still had a brain," she says, "and I decided that I'd get my master's degree in social work and become a therapist, specializing in the treatment of children."

Rose believes not only that Alma is responsible for her becoming a therapist but that she is a *better* therapist because of having her mentally disabled daughter in her life. "It opens your eyes to a whole other way of existing in the world," she says. "Watching how she suffers for being different gives me a great deal of empathy for suffering and difference, much more than I would have had otherwise, and enriches what I'm able to do as a therapist."

Alma had also enriched the life of her older sister—the one who, when she was little, wanted her mother to give Alma back. "She wants to do art therapy and has had jobs on and off during college at a camp for emotionally disturbed children," Rose says. "It's clear that Alma has impacted her life as well and made her somewhat of a defender of people who are different in any way. The simplicity of someone like Alma never sugarcoating anything and saying exactly what's on her mind has had an impact, too. As my older daughter says, 'She keeps us all honest.'"

Despite her difficulties with attachment to other people, Alma absolutely adores Rose. She reacts to her when she sees her as if she's her fairy godmother, the way a six- or seven-year-old would, and Rose loves Alma dearly. "If I had the chance to do it over," she says, "I'd do it again."

A Source of Powerful Motivation

An outside event may be the catalyst for jumping off one track and leaping onto another in order to follow your pattern, but it's the internal shift in your perception of yourself that provides the impetus to actually make the leap. Rose's realization that she "still had a brain" after she went back to college motivated her to go on to graduate school while she was raising two young children, one of them seriously disabled, and fulfill her dream of becoming a therapist. Rose's story is typical of how powerful your motivation is when an adversity knocks you into alignment with your true purpose in the world. People who are jolted into discovering and following their pattern often have the passionate perseverance to surmount obstacles that by anyone's standards seem insurmountable.

A client of my agency, for example, a middle-aged man facing a financial crisis after he was fired, was furious at his employer and terrified of the future. But then, his dream of starting his own online consulting business galvanized him into action. He drew up a business plan and went through dozens of frustrating meetings with potential investors without being able to raise a cent. Again and again he was told the same thing: The information highway is littered with the road kill of failed startup dot.coms. A heart attack and a triple bypass operation sidelined him for a month, but as soon as he was back on his feet, he began searching for backers again and finally found one. His first year as an entrepreneur was anxiety-filled but exhilarating as only the expression of your own creativity can be. In the second year, against all the odds, the business began to take off, and the man who once considered suing the employer who fired him is grateful to him now for giving him the chance to live out his entrepreneurial dream.

Another client, a thirty-eight-year-old married father of three children, had worked in the family business for seventeen years and was devastated by the death from cancer of his cousin, who was like a twin brother to him. Although our client was capable in business, his real passion was photography. The loss of his much-loved cousin aroused intimations of his own mortality, and he felt compelled to do what he really wanted to do with the rest of his life. In therapy he worked up the courage to leave his father's business, against his family's stiff opposition, and pursue his dream of making art out of the scenes and people he loved to photograph. He spent several frustrating years working for a commercial photographer to pay the bills while struggling to gain recognition as a serious photographic artist. Undaunted by rejection, he traveled to a book fair in Germany with a collection of his photographs to see if he could interest a publisher of art books in them. A publisher there was impressed with his work and offered him a contract after he got home. The book created a stir when it came out, leading to an exhibit of his work by an art studio. The photographs sold well, and he started picking up other work, gained the confidence to quit his day job and open his own studio, and went on to achieve success as a serious photographer.

Dreams as Signposts

Sometimes the calling is not a conscious yearning, as in the case of the corporate employee turned entrepreneur or the businessman whose passion was photography, but manifests itself in the form of a symbolic dream. A woman client came to the agency depressed about her recent divorce and disenchanted with the idea of taking an office job that she thought would become routine and boring.

Although she was grieving the loss of her marriage and worried about being a single parent, she felt ready to create a new life for herself. She wanted to find promising work that engaged her, but she wasn't sure where to look. In therapy she revealed a dream she kept having about a beautiful brooch her grandmother had left her when she died. She was looking for the brooch everywhere but couldn't find it and assumed it was stolen; yet when she awoke and went to look for the brooch, there it was in her jewelry box. Her grandmother, a gourmet cook and restaurateur, had passed her culinary skills along to her, and the dream seemed to be telling her that she was in danger of losing this other inherited "jewel" if she didn't develop it further. She had often toyed with the idea of doing more with her skills than entertaining friends at dinner parties, and now that her old social life was behind her, she saw this as her chance to turn her dilettantism into a career. Emboldened by her new dream, she went to culinary school, apprenticed as a sous chef, worked her way up to chef, and eventually opened her own restaurant, putting in sixteen-hours days to make it a success. Not only is she successful, she has also grown spiritually, donating free meals to homebound AIDS patients and contributing Thanksgiving dinners to homeless shelters as a way of paying back to the community for her good fortune.

As a pathway to the unconscious, dreams allow you to recognize not only a desire to move in a particular direction but also your hidden fears associated with making that move. Having your fears revealed to you in a dream gives you the chance to deal with them consciously instead of letting them rob you of the impetus to take the next step toward rebuilding your life. Recurrent "back-to-school" dreams, for example, are anxiety-driven dreams commonly experienced by someone contemplating an opportunity presented by a crisis. In these dreams a time warp has transported you back to your high school or college years at final exam time, and you are panic-stricken, trying to take an exam that you need to pass—or you will fail to graduate. You are seated at your desk in a classroom, desperately trying to answer impossible questions as the minutes on the clock tick by relentlessly. Or you've gotten lost on your way to the classroom and are racing frantically down the hall, searching for the room but never able to find it. Or you may arrive at the classroom and be told, to your consternation, that the test is already over.

What do these dreams mean? On the surface they would seem to indicate that you're still suffering anxiety about failing to graduate because of flunking some difficult test back in the days when you were a student. On a deeper level, these dreams are not about your fears of failing to graduate in the past but are a metaphor for your concerns about "graduating" in real life today—taking the next step and actually implementing the possibility you envisage for yourself. You fear that you don't have the wherewithal to find or succeed at a new job or to start your own business or to be happy in love or to raise a family as a single parent or to go on to a higher level of education or to take any kind of risk that could bring you more fulfillment.

These dreams are representations of the normal fears and doubts that anyone about to undertake a new challenge experiences, but they are also reminders of the goals you have for yourself. Look your fears in the face, and deny them the power to stop you. Take them as a call to move in tandem with your higher self and become more of who you are. You cannot lose if you choose to leap without a safety net, knowing that you'll receive what you need for your growth and, should you happen to fall, will bounce back and climb higher. No risk is unreasonable if it leads you to where you need to be. When you act on the call of your soul, your anxiety dreams will stop, because you are creating a new dream in real life. By doing the thing you fear you can't do, you'll gain in courage and confidence and discover that you're a much stronger person than you thought. You'll come to know a more profound dimension of yourself that would have remained undiscovered had you not pushed through the barriers of your fears.

> No risk is unreasonable if it leads you to where you need to be.

Taking the Plunge

Before we commit to a new possibility after the collapse of what we've known, many of us torture ourselves trying to figure out all the angles. We get stuck in the evaluation phase of the creative process, turning our decision this way and that, second-guessing ourselves, dizzily weighing the pros and cons like someone trying to follow the little white ball in a ping-pong match.

The fact is that none of us can ever comprehend all of the factors involved in an important decision. We can go on balancing the pros against the cons forever and not be able to arrive at a fail-safe conclusion. We can't possibly know all the answers. Why? Because we live in a world limited by our five senses and don't have access to the source of unlimited knowledge in the metaphysical world. The research that we do—reading books and magazines, surfing the Internet, asking people for advice—can't take us beyond the bounds of our physical limitations and rational minds.

The closest we can get to the metaphysical world is through our insight and intuition, the deeply felt sense that this is what we *must* do, that what we want to do is right for us, that it fits our soul, not only our self-image. Doubt is the enemy of creativity. At some point we have to push the off button on all our data gathering and processing and just take the plunge, having the total certainty that it's going to work out to our benefit in the long run. When we surrender our illusion of omniscience to an intelligence much greater than our own—an intelligence that created the universe and all of human life—we will be astonished by what we can accomplish.

Taking the plunge with total certainty—the "believing is seeing" principle—lets your creativity operate without the dead weight of doubt and anxiety. Pursuing your dream is not about being right or wrong; it's about growth and transformation, connecting to a higher power within and without, and raising up your own worth by contributing something of value to others. When you come from that place of wanting to give of yourself to others instead of a "what's in it for me" mentality, you automatically connect to a flow of positive, creative energy, and synchronicities begin to happen. Without your ego blocking that energy from you, it will work its magic. You'll find yourself in the right place at the right time or you'll

Pursuing your dream is not about being right or wrong; it's about growth and transformation.

meet the right person to support your growth or doors will open for you that all your anxious, driven, desperate pounding on before wouldn't budge. As a result, you'll take a giant step toward recognizing your truest self and your own personal destiny.

The Birth of a New Dream

The breakup of my first marriage in the early 1970s forced me, as it does so many other suddenly single mothers, to create a new identity and a new dream. During my marriage I had already begun searching for a career and started out as a comedy writer, lampooning my life as a doctor's wife. The publisher of my second book, a novel satirizing the dirty book business, offered me a three-book contract even before that one came out. I started to write the first of the three, a spoof of *The Exorcist* called *Mrs. Katz's Demon,* but I wasn't feeling very funny at the time. The age of feminism was dawning and had stirred up a desire in me to be taken seriously. While I enjoyed making people laugh, I wanted to say more than I thought comedy writing would allow, and I relinquished my publishing contract.

It was a decision that came back to haunt me. I embarked on a frustrating period of racing around and around in an anxiety rut, frantically, ceaselessly striving for career success, but somehow always programming myself for failure. An ill-conceived book project I worked on for two years never materialized. The TV pilot I struggled to get on the air, investing more years of compulsive effort, never found a home. When a movie deal on a screenplay I'd written fell through, I plunged into despair. Meanwhile, the fault line in my marriage grew wider and wider from these years of rushing around, trying to gain recognition as a writer and break into broadcasting, and the marital bond finally cracked wide open.

Grappling with my marriage's demise, I began to reevaluate the choices I'd made in my life. I realized that I married my husband for all the wrong reasons—financial security, status, to be taken care of—and I sadly had to admit that although there was once genuine love, we were ill-suited to each other. The marriage came to a bitter end. When we separated, I was frightened and confused about the future and hounded by anxiety. I felt like a hapless cork bobbing in a sea of uncertainty. I had a total of $15,000 in the bank and two young children to raise—and no job. I stayed awake nights, chewing my fingernails. Faced with the cold, hard reality of having to make a living, I gave up all my notions of instant fame and overnight bestsellerdom and applied to law school. I made up my mind that I needed a career that offered security rather than the uncertain rewards of pursuing my craft as a writer.

About the same time that I was accepted for admission to law school, an idea for yet another book, this one a serious work about how women had been swallowed up by their roles in marriage, was taking shape in my mind. Oh, no, not again, I said to myself, you're going to law school, remember? But the book cried out to be written, and the idea wouldn't go away. Before putting anything down on paper, I wanted to test out my perspective and talk to other women in the same straits with their marriages as I was. I called a friend of mine, a children's author, with the idea of collaborating on the book, and we took a walk in the park to brainstorm. It was an autumn day with a wintry feel, and we were trudging through piles of fallen leaves when the idea came to me—a marital hotline.

Maverick that I was, I didn't want to research the book the conventional way. Instead, I wanted to reach out to women throughout the whole Delaware Valley in Pennsylvania and have them call in with their problems so that we could listen empathetically and offer support and guidance. Helping other women through an anonymous telephone call-in service—I didn't even know enough to call it a hotline then—seemed like such a powerful thing to do that it took precedence over writing the book. I didn't care whether a book grew out of it or not. Uncharacteristically for me, I wanted to do the hotline simply because the mountain was there, not climb it to make myself feel taller.

My friend loved the idea and offered to help me launch it, but as soon as it popped out of my mouth, I began to have second thoughts. Doubt, the enemy of creativity, reared its inimical head. I got caught up in my usual risk-averse, logical thinking, trying to take everything into account that might lead to failure. For hours I went through every reason not to go ahead with the project, all the things I could think of that could possibly go wrong. Like everyone else preparing to take a different direction in life, I also questioned my motivations. Would I be giving up on law school because I thought I didn't have what it took to succeed? Finally, I stopped second-guessing myself and decided to take a leap of faith—no, of *certainty*—that I would do what I had to do for the sake of my soul, and it would all turn out somehow. Deep down I felt that becoming a lawyer was a false calling for me, a profession I was drawn to for the status and financial security, not a choice from the heart. By starting the hotline I wasn't running away; I was running toward my truest self and my own personal destiny.

The hotline, called Wives Self Help, started out in my friend's bedroom—an apt place for a marital hotline—and immediately took off beyond anything I could have imagined. For the first time in my life I was doing something as an act of simple giving, and the universe responded in kind. A press release sent out to the local media, which I thought would be tossed in the trashcan, brought TV crews and newspaper reporters flocking to the bedroom. Soon there was national coverage, and *Donahue*, then the hottest show in all of daytime television, was calling. It seemed like every other TV and radio show in the country followed suit, and Wives Self Help achieved fame as the first marital hotline in America.

A group of close friends helped me quickly cobble together a cadre of other volunteers. We had everyone trained by a psychologist, and we set up a referral system and moved operations into a room donated by a church. A fundraiser brought enough money to move into a two-room space above an optician's office. Then came a grant from the city to counsel police officers and their wives, together with another move into a high-rise building.

None of this would have happened without the training to develop skills, plenty of hard work, patient attention to details, and the inch-by-inch gaining of confidence and know-how from piling one small success on top of another. The universe was on our side in keeping the dream alive, but only because we had the willingness to battle fiercely whenever it was threatened with extinction. Eventually, the hotline burgeoned into a full-fledged professional mental health counseling agency for men, women, and children, with a large staff, including three psychiatrists, helping thousands of people improve their lives over the years, and is still going strong today.

Wives Self Help struck a deep nerve in the public at a time when the feminist movement was having a big impact on traditional marriage, but for me, personally, it was a watershed experience. Out of one of the worst times in my life came this call from my soul to be true to myself, to be faithful to the honest-to-God me and do things in my own way, not anyone else's. I had no inkling of how the hotline would be perceived. Maybe people would laugh at me for coming out of the closet with my marital problems or question my authority to give advice to other people. I also had no concept of how this project would ever make money. But none of that mattered to me. All I knew was that this was something I had to do—the mission in life that I was called upon to fulfill.

Because I started Wives Self Help with no other intention than reaching out to others and sharing and giving, I connected with the Field of Answered Prayers on the right basis. Ironically, I received all the rewards and recognition that were denied me when I was desperately seeking them before. Answering countless hotline calls from troubled women brought me a wealth of firsthand material and valuable knowledge that resulted in a book, a radio show, and a position as a contributing editor for a national magazine. But these payoffs were an outgrowth of doing the thing I loved, not the reason for doing it. I "backed into" success when I stopped frantically wasting my energy trying to become the person I thought I *should* be and enlisted the energy of the universe to help me make the most of the person I actually am.

Getting What You Need

Founding Wives Self Help proved to me what a marvelous thing the absence of ego is when you're creating a new dream out of the wreckage of your old life. The cardinal rule I learned is this: Your driving dream should be to fulfill your purpose in life, not expect life to fulfill you. You can achieve greatly beyond the norm when you're driven by selfish concerns, but your insecurity will never go away. Over-involvement with your own ego imprisons you in a spiritual vacuum, causes your relationships to suffer, and keeps you in a constant state of striving for more and more and never feeling fulfilled. On the other hand, when you're pursuing your dream because you want to give of the best within you, setbacks will not devastate you, and your relationships will sustain you as you keep moving forward toward your goals in a balanced way. Regardless of your achievements, in time, looking back at the person you've become, you'll be able to say, "I've lived a good life."

Pursuing your new dream in any area of your life—your job or career ambitions or your personal goals, such as **Your driving dream should be to fulfill your pupose in life, not expect life to fulfill you.** finding a committed relationship or having a happy marriage and family life—demands that you ride through your fear of failure. The tremendous emphasis our culture puts on successes and achievements ignores the fact that falling down and rising up again is the central theme of the story of the human race. You can't get in touch with your true purpose in life and acquire the wisdom and courage to pursue it without the mistakes and failures and losses that point you in the right direction and develop your inner strength.

The real mistake is to think, as I once did, that by exerting enough pressure you can push your way to the top in one bold maneuver and thereby eliminate the slow, painful process of growth. Not only do you need to recognize your failures as friends that will help you grow spiritually; you also need to shift your focus away from the end result to learning from the questions. A familiar example I've encountered is the woman who chases a man away by pressing for a commitment before the relationship has weathered all the ups and downs that lead to the attainment of genuine intimacy. If she were willing to endure the hard times and let the relationship unfold, she could learn how to make it work, or failing that, learn enough so that the next relationship has a better chance of fulfilling her dream of commitment. The same is true in business, in the development of talent, and in the pursuit of happiness. Very often, getting what you want comes at the end of the long, bumpy, trial-and-error road of getting what you need.

I'm reminded of a blind man I saw walking with a cane down Beach Boulevard in Fort Lauderdale, Florida, along with the roller bladers, joggers, and other strollers enjoying a beautiful day near the ocean. Approaching a large tree in his path, the blind man tapped the front of the trunk with his cane, tapped the sides to ascertain it's parameters, and then skillfully sidestepped the massive obstacle in his path and continued on his way. In a sense, we're all blind travelers on our journey through life, and the obstacles we encounter are not meant to stop us but to help us learn what we need to know in order to arrive at our destination. The years we put into a failed dream are never wasted. They're the rich loam in which we cultivate our ultimate triumphs. Knowing that, we can never let our fear of failure stop us from risking a new dream.

Sometimes you simply have to live your life like an unsolved riddle, not fully understanding how to make sense of it, until some crisis unlocks the mystery and reveals your true purpose to you. Carol is an example of someone who found her mission in life in just that way.

Carol

When Nick Ide walked into Carol Seelaus's apartment in 1991 for a meeting of her short story writers' group, she was thirty-seven and had never been married. Nick, who was thirty-four and also single, had called her for a date and told her he wanted to do some writing. Put off by his monotone voice, she invited him to the meeting, not expecting anything to come of it. Her girlfriend sitting next to her cast an appraising eye over this tall, blond, buff guy, who was not only "gorgeous" but also had a master's degree in physics, and said under her breath, "Thank you, God."

For Carol and Nick, it was a meeting of kindred souls. They had both suffered considerable emotional deprivation growing up and were searching for meaning in their lives. They found it in each other and were together for six years, hiking, cooking gourmet meals, bird-watching, spending winter weekends sledding and snuggling in rustic cabins in the countryside. Over a romantic dinner one night, Nick picked up two floating candles, held them flame to flame until they merged, and said, "That's us." Carol, an attractive, slim, open-hearted woman, the kind you'd like to have for a best friend, says, "I think the reason Nick and I got together when I was thirty-seven is that we really needed each other to find out what was going on. We were a perfect match. We didn't take away from the other one's personality. We kind of grew into what we were supposed to be together."

On a Sunday in October 1997, Nick was helping friends put a new roof on their Victorian home when the forty-foot extension ladder he was standing on fell, taking him down with it. Carol got the call to come to the hospital late at night. "I was afraid he was going to die," she says, "and on the way over I kept saying goodbye to him." Nick survived, but he emerged from a six-week coma severely brain-injured and quadriplegic. He was given an 84 percent chance of remaining in a permanent vegetative state. While he was still in the emergency room, Carol asked Nick if he wanted to die. He shook his head no. And that's when Carol knew what her mission in life was. As long as Nick wanted to stay alive, she would be there to help him live.

In the years that followed, Carol's unflagging devotion to Nick had her friends and even seasoned medical professionals shaking their heads in wonderment. She was with Nick five days a week, four to six hours at a time—reading to him, singing to him, propping him up when he slid down in bed, showering him with kisses. As surgeries and infections kept him shuttling back and forth among hospitals, nursing homes, and rehabs, Carol moved from place to place to be close to him. She lost half her income as the owner of a house cleaning company called Somebody's Gotta Do It, but she never lost a speck of the love and affection she felt for Nick before he fell. In fact, her bond with him grew even stronger as she assumed the role of impassioned advocate, fighting to make insurance companies, medical people, social workers, and assorted bureaucrats care about what happened to him.

Every so often people would ask Carol why, when she wasn't married to Nick, she was devoting her life to him so selflessly. They would say, "You know, you could turn around and leave him at any time." She told them, "No! I love him! I chose to do this. I do it willingly." Even before Nick's accident, as Carol entered her forties still single, people would ask her, "Don't you want to get married? Don't you want to have children?" Carol didn't. "I never really understood why getting married and having children had never been a priority for me," she says. "And then, when Nick fell, I knew why. If he and I had gotten married and had children, then it would have diluted the help that I would have been able to give him. People question why they are on this earth. This is why I'm here. I really believe that. This feels so right."

Describing herself as a "lapsed Catholic," Carol says she learned how to trust in a power greater than herself in the early going when the hospital was discharging Nick to go die in a nursing home (if he died in the hospital, the insurance company wouldn't pay for it). She went into the chapel and wrote in the prayer book, "Dear God, please tell me what to do about Nick." It wasn't, "Please make Nick better" or "Please put Nick out of his misery," just, "Please tell me what to do." Carol explains, "If you're just really, really quiet inside, and you don't get all balled up into yourself and your life and don't feel like you're fighting whatever it is, something kind of tells you or guides you into what to do."

> **"People question why they are on this earth. This is why I'm here. This feels so right."**

It was Carol who saw subtle signs that Nick was coming back when he was in rehab, but his HMO decided that he would have to be sent to a nursing home. He lay there, flat on his back, staring at the ceiling, another forgotten victim of warehousing, able to communicate only by raising his eyebrows. When the nursing home wouldn't put him in a wheelchair, Carol had an inspiration. She contacted a newspaper writer who'd done a series on nursing homes and asked him to come out and see Nick. The subsequent article caught the attention of a facility called Inglis House, and Nick was accepted into their wheelchair community. He started to improve and steadily kept on going. He didn't retain his personality, but this personality, according to Carol, is far more lovable than the old one was. "Before his injury he was like a square peg, very cerebral and very shy and would go to a party and sit in the corner," she says. "Now he has a sense of humor and loves to talk to people. He'll drive out in the yard at Inglis House and wave to everybody and say hello to everybody and engage everybody in conversation. I tell him, 'You know, you're turning into me.'"

On September 22, 2001, Carol and Nick became "life partners" in a moving commitment ceremony held on the grounds of Inglis House. Carol didn't want to become Nick's wife because she was afraid that any change in her status as his legal guardian would diminish her effectiveness as his protector and advocate. By the time of the ceremony Nick was able to drive himself around in his power wheelchair, whisper a few words, use his left hand, play a wicked game of chess, and type with a communication device, on which he wrote his vows and would tell Carol things like, "The times I spend with you are idyllic" and "I love you more than life itself."

Throughout the ceremony Carol held Nick's hand, beaming and weeping at the same time. She spent that night with Nick in his bed for the first time in many months. He fell asleep as soon as his head hit the pillow, but when he woke up in the morning and realized he wasn't alone, he turned his head toward Carol and gave her a magnificent smile. "We can hold each other, but we haven't tried to have a physical relationship," she says. "He's on antidepressant medication that might make it difficult for him. I think he would be capable of it if I pursued it, but I'm not pursuing it because I don't want him to think that there's another thing he can't do."

This may strike some people as martyrdom, but Carol says that's only because they don't understand what Nick gives back to her. "He gives me a little electrical charge whenever I go into his room," she says. "When we're just sitting together, holding each other and listening to music, there is no place I'd rather be. Before Nick fell, I was head-ing toward understanding what's really important in life, and now I think I have that knowledge. Being there for somebody I love and *wanting* to be there is my highest priority. It has nothing to do with 'duty.' I don't drag my ass over to visit him; I fly there. I told Nick, if I die before you, I'm coming back to haunt you. And if you go, you're going to have to keep me company."

Besides finding her life's purpose in loving and sustaining Nick and empowering him to get better, Carol thinks she was meant to be teaching people through her life, too. On Nick's Web site, designed free of charge by a boyhood friend of his, Carol maintains a running log of the struggles and triumphs in Nick's recovery, dispenses morsels of homespun wisdom, relates friends' stories, and answers everyone who signs the guest book. "I want people to know that some things have to get really bad before they get good again," she says. "We have to hold onto that and listen, not try to engineer everything, but just experience it, and we'll figure out the right thing to do. I have no regrets."

Just as Carol found in adversity the revelation of her true purpose in life, the one right thing for her to do, the choice from her heart, so can we all. The path she chose may not be right for you, given similar circumstances, but her feelings about the choice and her way of arriving at all the other important choices in her life are what matters. If you quiet the chattering of your fears and the chorus of outside opinion and pay attention to your own inner voice, you can find your calling in any sphere of life that matters most to you—intimate love, family, work, artistic expression, achievements, personal development. As Marc Gaffney says so beautifully in his book *Soul Prints*, "Listen deeply and transform what may appear to be the fate of the lottery into the destiny of the soul."

Strength-Building Exercise:
"Find Your Direction"

This exercise will help you choose from among the possibilities you've identified in the previous chapter and create a new dream for yourself by finding clues to your true purpose and letting your intuition and insights guide you toward it.

- List anything that touched you deeply—a movie scene, a book, a recurring dream, an incident, a conversation, a lecture, a tape—and write down what meaning you think it has for you. What is it trying to tell you about why you are here on this earth, how you should live your life, and what your next step should be?
- Pretend you're a contestant on a television quiz show, and the million-dollar question is, "What is your life all about?" How would you answer?
- Spend some time each day when you can be alone with your thoughts—meditating, doing yoga, walking, or listening to music. Write down any insights that come to you during these activities and ask if they are guiding you toward any particular goal.
- Make a list of the things you've done in your life that have made you feel most proud or worthwhile or have given you the most pleasure. What can you do now that will give you that same feeling of gratification?
- Ask yourself how you would most like to be remembered in life after you're gone, and write down your answer.

- If you had to pick one thing you're really good at, what would it be? Where is there a need for that skill in the world today? Which of your possibilities gives you an opportunity to employ that skill in a way you would most enjoy?
- Was there some dream you gave up in the past because it wasn't practical? If you still dream of doing it, can you go about it responsibly now?
- If taking a big risk frightens you, try taking smaller ones—experiment with a new recipe, give a talk in public, make a social engagement with someone new. If the adventure doesn't work out the way you hoped, focus on what would make it better next time. Work on developing a forgiving attitude toward mistakes or failures, not as missteps to be looked back upon with shame or regret, but as helpful guideposts to the future.
- Draw up a plan of action to implement your new dream and give you a feeling of control over this next stage of your life. Make your plan as detailed as possible. What resources will you need, and how can you get them? Are there people you can call upon to help you bring your dream to life? What steps do you have to take to set it in motion? Take the first step now!

Part IV

Regeneration

9

Love Doesn't Leave

Some people believe that death is only an illusion—people who die are no longer here in this physical world, but their souls rejoin the creative energy of the universe and live on eternally in the unseen spiritual world. According to the ancients, this whole world is just illusory, the dream from which death awakens us. This realization, said the Tibetan Buddhists, will help us abandon all our worldly grasping and attachment when the moment of death comes and, in the form of radiant light, enter into the clear awareness of enlightenment.

Whether you share this belief in death as a transition or believe it's the absolute end, I think you know that death ends the life of a loved one but never ends the love that existed in that relationship. Love outlasts death and still travels with us, making us what we are and will become. Rudolph Giuliani, then mayor of New York, said it all when he tried to console a young boy standing with his hand over his heart, fighting back tears at the funeral of his police officer father who was killed in the World Trade Center tragedy. "Your daddy didn't leave you," Giuliani told the boy. "All the things you loved about him are inside you."

By the same token, you never "get over" the loss of the person either. Loss is not something you put aside like the newspaper after you've finished reading it. You accommodate loss and integrate it into your life, but no one should expect

Love outlasts death and still travels with us, making us what we are and will become.

you, least of all yourself, to sever the emotional ties you had with the person who is gone, get on with your life, and never look back. The death of a loved one changes you forever. You're not the same person you were when you were the spouse of the person who died or the mother of the child who was killed or the sibling of the brother or sister who passed away. As we've seen, accepting loss means letting go of who you were in a previous relationship and of the life you had with that person, but that doesn't mean you let go of that person's legacy. The cultural notion that it's unhealthy to maintain a connection to a loved one who has died after a certain point is absurd. Actually, it's unhealthy *not* to maintain that connection by talking about the person and creating memorial rituals, customs, or other kinds of remembrances, because cutting the ties forces your pain and sorrow underground, only to resurface later in physical or emotional illness.

Staying Connected After Death

Commemorating your loved one provides you with an ongoing source of comfort and an impetus to honor that person's memory through achievements that stretch you farther than you thought you could go. As an avid baseball fan, I remember watching Curt Schilling, the brilliant Arizona Diamondbacks pitcher pitch a flawless game one night in the 2001

World Series. At one point, the camera cut from the pitching mound to a shot of an empty seat beside Schilling's wife. The announcer explained that Schilling always leaves an empty seat next to his wife in honor of his father, Carl, who died in 1988. I have no doubt that the presence of his father's spirit in that seat is a big factor in Schilling's success.

Another vignette of someone maintaining ties with a beloved family member after death is a more personal one. My youngest stepchild, Susan, was a teenager when her grandfather died, and she was one of the pallbearers at his funeral. To feel that he was still a part of her and always would be, she put on an old overcoat of her grandfather's before she took her place beside his casket. I'll never forget the image of this young girl, walking with her head bowed and her pretty features crumpled into the face of grief, her grandfather's coat enveloping her in a symbolic bear hug as she helped carry him away. Even in death he was able to comfort her.

Keeping tangible remembrances of someone we've lost not only motivates us to recover from our grief and live our lives to the fullest in the loved one's honor; it also ensures that person's immortality in the world left behind. The faded photographs, the videos, the letters, the journals, the personal effects and other mementoes that spark reminiscences ensure that our loved one will continue to influence and enrich the lives of others for generation after generation beyond the grave. When we don't let death snuff out our connections to a loved one, we know that we, too, can live on in the lives of those we've loved in a lasting and significant way after we die. People leave. Love doesn't.

The media attention focused on some of the widows of the Twin Tower heroes who were killed trying to save others brought an exciting and temporary distraction from their grief and loneliness. But away from the hot glare of the media spotlight, they struggled like all the other widows to find a new way of living in the world without their spouses and to ease the pain of their suddenly fatherless children. Suzanne Berger was left to raise her three boys, two, six, and eight, when her husband, James Berger, a forty-four-year-old insurance executive, died after evacuating most of his 125 coworkers on his floor in the South Tower. Chosen to carry the Olympic torch in her husband's honor through Philadelphia on December 22, 2001, Suzanne, a former pediatric nurse, said in a *Philadelphia Inquirer* interview, "I want people to look on us and see hope."

In a previous interview Suzanne revealed how difficult it had been for her three young sons to adjust to their father's death. The oldest boy, Nicholas, was angry at his father for saving others but not himself and thought he might have upset his dad the weekend before and caused him not to get in the elevator and go down to safety. Her middle son, Alexander, began acting up during quiet time in school, because quiet time made him have to think about his father and the World Trade Center. Christian, the toddler, screamed out for his father in the middle of the night.

With the help of a therapist for the two older boys, the family began to cope. Suzanne would talk with Nicholas and Alexander at bedtime about their favorite memories of their father and ask him to watch over them, and the boys began carrying around a wallet with their father's photograph in it. Feeling their father as an ongoing, loving, and protective presence in their lives helped redirect Nicholas's anger into more positive outlets and improve Alexander's behavior at school. Christian started sleeping much better at night as he, too, found a way to maintain a connection with his father. Suzanne overheard him talking to his father when he first awakened in the morning as if his daddy were lying beside him in bed. During the day he would turn to Suzanne sometimes and ask her if she knew his Daddy had died, then quickly reassure her, saying, "It's OK. He's in heaven with angels."

Children who have lost their parents or siblings but are encouraged to commemorate them have an appreciation of life that they didn't have before. Having been made aware of death as part of the life cycle, as something that is going to happen to everyone, they have a greater respect for life and are less likely to flirt with danger. They also see that even with all the pain and sadness they feel, love goes on and so does life. Finding that they can still have friends, go to school, engage in activities they like and have fun, they develop the survivor attitude: I can handle this and whatever comes next.

Chasing Closure

The notion of "closure"—that definitive moment when bereaved people are supposed to be able to close the book on their suffering and put their loss behind them—is elusive at best and can even be harmful. Timothy McVeigh's execution did not make the relatives of victims killed in the Oklahoma City bombing feel at peace with their loss. Family members who lost loved ones in the attacks on the Twin Towers did not feel an ending to their grief and pain when they were given an urn filled with ashes from the site or received death certificates or had bodies returned to them that others didn't have. No memorial or climactic act of retribution or justice wipes away grief any more than it puts an end to the disaffection that causes terrorists and other criminals to take the lives of innocent people. To hope for such immediate closure or chase after it is to set yourself up for disappointment. Memorials offer solace, justice provides some small sense of fairness, and a burial makes a loved one's death more real than watching a heinous event on the TV news, but these acts do not solve everything.

Chasing after closure is a hunt for the false promise that things will return to normal as soon as you come face-to-face with reality. Although you need to confront the reality of death before you can begin to integrate it into your life, confronting it is the beginning of healing, not the ending of grief as the word *closure* implies. The expectation that emotions should run on schedule like a train is a symptom of a society that has no tolerance for tears and believes that everyone should get back to normal as soon as possible. Mourning has to run its course. The whole concept of closure underestimates the impact of death on people and the length of time some of us have to struggle with its different aspects and effects until we can finally assimilate it. Closure is not something to pursue as an end in itself; it's a consequence of acceptance—letting go of what you once had, while still remembering and honoring the joy it gave you, and allowing the joy to exceed the pain of losing it.

Frank and Janet are an example of bereaved parents who were able to accept the loss of their daughter to an unthinkable act of brutality, even though they were denied any possibility of closure in the usual sense of the word. They were inconsolable when their nineteen-year-old daughter, Melissa, a college student, was raped and murdered by an intruder who broke into the apartment she was living in off campus. "It

> **Closure is not something to pursue as an end in itself; it's a consequence of acceptance.**

broke our hearts that we never got a chance to say goodbye to her," Janet says. "The thought of her dying like that, so savagely, all alone with no one to help her, was unbearable. They never caught the man who did it, and that made it even worse. It was terrifying to think he was on the loose and might do the same thing to someone else's child."

The couple found solace from their local chapter of Parents of Murdered Children, an organization that helps survivors deal with their grief as well as with the criminal justice system. "Those weekly meetings saved our sanity," Frank says. "They helped us let go of some of our rage and frustration and the idea that we could have saved Melissa's life if we insisted that she live in the dorm. We all think we're supposed to keep our children out of harm's way, but you can't protect them from everything. You can't stop life from happening no matter what you do."

Describing the self-help weekend they went to as a "breakthrough," Janet says, "Until then, we were eating ourselves up alive with hate and a desire for revenge, or at least retribution. We wanted her killer brought to justice, but that wasn't going to bring Melissa back. Nothing was ever going to change that. We saw our pain mirrored in the faces of the other people there, and they finally got through to us and helped us realize how useless hate and revenge were. There's that moment of truth when you stop screaming inside and you're able to say, 'It is what it is; let's go on from here.'" Frank adds, "We turned a corner with our grief when we decided to focus on the love and affection we had for Melissa that nothing, not even death, could take away. We came home determined to celebrate Melissa's life and keep her spirit alive, keep her a part of our family always, in concrete ways."

One of the ways Frank and Janet maintained their connection with Melissa was by writing letters to her in a journal observing significant occasions: birthdays, graduations, weddings, the anniversary of her death. They embellished the journal with photos and drawings, some done by Melissa herself before a senseless act of violence ended her hopes of becoming an illustrator of children's books some day. They also included Melissa in every important family event. At his graduation ceremony from high school, Ryan, her younger brother, gave a moving valedictory speech in her honor. He said that she would always be a role model for him to develop his own potential and that her death taught him to value every day of his life. Later that day, Ryan went to the cemetery with the speech encased in a plastic folder and dug a spot for it in front of Melissa's grave.

Symbolic Signs

People who concentrate on keeping the legacy of their loved one alive sometimes find encouragement in perceived messages from the dead person in dreams or synchronous events. Beth, for example, whose husband, Marc, died in a plane crash shortly after their third child was born, had a recurring dream of trying to find him, chasing after him, desperately trying to grab hold of his hand, and having him elude her and disappear. "I think the dream epitomized my feelings of pain, helplessness, and fear," she says, "but I knew Marc would want me to go on as if he were still with us, carrying on his influence in our daily lives. He was a happy person with a lot of interests: He loved going on camping trips with our boys, he liked to cook, he played guitar. He felt that life was meant to be enjoyed, and I wanted to impart that attitude to our kids."

Whenever Beth felt crushed by grief and the burden of going it alone, something unexpected—some sign, some symbol—would remind her that Marc's spirit was still with her. "One morning, after the older children left for school, I was walking down the street, wheeling the baby in her carriage, seeing Marc in my mind, and I lost it. I starting shouting furiously, *'How could you have left us? How could you!'* I was so mad. All of a sudden a township police car drove up, and an officer came out, and he said, 'Are you okay?' I guess he saw me crying. I said, 'I'm just in a lot of pain. My husband died.' And the officer said, 'Well, if you ever need anything, let me give you my card.' He handed me his card, and I was dumbfounded. His name was the same as my husband's—the exact same spelling, same last name, same middle initial!"

That incident, Beth says, made her feel that Marc hadn't left her after all. He was still with her spiritually, and she drew strength from their connection. Her dreams started to change. When she reached out for him, he didn't elude her any more. Instead, he stopped to talk with her, gave her comfort and advice. "I worked a lot out in my dreams," Beth says, "and I learned that even in death, the person you love is still there for you, loving you back, supporting you, helping you rebuild your life and move forward."

Setting an Example: Sandy and Judy

People who've developed strategies for celebrating life even when life is hard set an example for their children by the way they accept every calamity, including the death of a loved one, with grace. Sandy Toll, an exemplar of the principle of unconditional happiness that I described in Chapter 5, has been an inspiring role model for her daughter, comedy writer and performer, Judy Toll. Judy has had to cope not only with her father's death but also with her own serious illness. The story of this mother and daughter and the important people in their lives has much to tell us about finding the inner strength to sustain us through the worst of times.

Sandy and her husband, Jay, were classmates of mine in high school. They were the storybook high school sweethearts—she the fair-skinned, cute blonde and he the darkly handsome popular guy—who married each other, had three children, and stayed together in a close, loving marriage for forty-five years. Periodically, Sandy and I would get together with some other committee members to plan our class reunions. We were getting ready to meet once again when someone on the committee called me up to tell me Jay had died. I was shocked, having heard that he'd just been through two successful surgeries, but I was told that complications from his chronic lung disease claimed his life. The day after I got the news, I steeled myself all morning to make a condolence call to Sandy that I thought would be a sad, painful matter. I couldn't imagine what it was like for her, losing her husband unexpectedly and having her oldest child, Judy, too sick to attend the funeral. On the day Jay died, Judy was in the hospital in Los Angeles, where she lives, being operated on for the tenth time for the melanoma she'd been diagnosed with several years before.

To my surprise and relief, Sandy was remarkably upbeat when I spoke to her. She said her family had always used humor to keep themselves going and that Jay's funeral was probably the only one people walked away from not feeling depressed. Instead of a eulogy, her son, Gary, and younger daughter, Joanne, delivered an amusing poem, poking gentle fun at their father's foibles while expressing their love for him. Sandy revealed that as frightened and worried as they were when Jay's condition worsened and he was in the intensive care unit, the family kept bouncing stories off one another, recalling funny incidents from their shared history, and ended up laughing. She remembered Lew, a close family friend and retired physician, coming to the hospital every day to make sure this wasn't going to be a "morbid death watch." Finally he said, "I guess I'll have to go home and grieve—I certainly can't do it here."

Describing the military burial her brother arranged for Jay, who'd been a marine as a young man, as "marvelous," Sandy said, "The flag draped the coffin, and a Marine Corps honor guard stood on either side of it throughout the whole service. At the end they took the flag off, folded it, and handed it to me and played taps, and it was magnificent, just so beautiful. My brother said there wasn't a dry eye in the place—except for me. It wasn't until we were leaving the cemetery and a friend of mine from college came up to me and hugged me that the flood gates opened up."

Sandy spoke glowingly about Judy's wedding five months before, a stellar event that took place when Jay seemed healthy. At forty-three, after a legendary, frustrating, no-stone-unturned search for a husband that found its way into her comedy sets on stage, Judy married Richard (Rick) Trank, an Academy Award–winning documentary film-maker and, in Sandy's words, "a phenomenal nurturer, an angel sent from heaven." After they were together only five months, Judy got the diagnosis that the melanoma she thought was cured had recurred. By then Rick was deeply in love with Judy, and his desire to marry her was not affected in the least by this unexpected turn of events. The night they came home from the hospital after her surgical procedure, Rick proposed, saying, "I want to spend the rest of my life with you." Since then he has been a model of devotion, even giving Judy her needles and performing other kinds of at-home medical care—this despite, as he tells it, having to pay a friend to cut up the frog for him in biology class when he was in high school.

Proud of her daughter's talent and spunk, Sandy told me how well Judy was doing in her job as a writer for the HBO hit show *Sex and the City*. After her last operation to remove a tumor in her leg, she was still going in to work, on crutches, three days a week. "Judy is a people magnet," Sandy said. "Everyone connected with the show loves her. She offered to quit, but they wouldn't hear of it."

The longer I spoke to her, the more aware I became that Sandy Toll, who seemed like everybody's next-door neighbor, was a remarkable woman who had a gift for counting her blessings when most other people would have been cursing their bad luck. What was her secret? What was the source of her unflagging emphasis on the positive? Had she always been this way?

It turns out that Sandy's childhood was hardly the ideal training ground for developing a sunny outlook—her mother was in and out of mental institutions for severe depression the whole time Sandy was growing up. "My father raised my brother and me by himself," she says, "and he was very affectionate and loving, but he was very strict. He scared the hell out of me. At the time I thought he was being mean, but I realize now what that man was made of and what he went through. He never complained, and he just expected us to do what we had to do, too. He was a good role model for us."

Sandy's father had a role model for resilience in his own father, whose wife died in childbirth after delivering their fifth child. "What are you going to do?" commiserating people asked the bereaved husband and newly single parent of five children. His answer was, "What am I going to do? I'm going to roll up my sleeves and get to work." Sandy remembers her father always saying, "You're put on this earth to suffer. If you have a good day, you have to be really thankful." She says, "That sounds pessimistic, but it isn't. Most of us are just expecting the happy times. But if you lower your expectations of the world, the bad times won't throw you so much, and you'll be really elated when something good happens."

Although Sandy's father had probably never heard of the Buddha, his philosophy is akin to the Buddhist teaching that suffering is a natural fact of human life—all flesh is heir to aging, illness, and death—and the freedom of no expectations is an antidote to despair. We can't expect to get through life without suffering, because suffering is what gives value to the gift of life—just as death is what makes life important. If we can adopt a tolerant attitude toward suffering instead of our usual hatred of it, the Dalai Lama tells us, we can defuse our feelings of unhappiness and unfairness and cope much better with suffering when it arises. A tolerant attitude toward suffering frees us from agonizing

Suffering is what gives value to the gift of life.

over it and allows us to confront the situation directly and focus on finding a solution to it.

Putting her father's philosophy into practice did not come easily for Sandy. Judy describes her mother as very "stressed out" when her children were young and constantly squabbling with each other. "I remember her getting hysterical, crying, and becoming really high strung," Judy says. "What happened was, she decided she wanted to change. She started reading books by parenting experts and watching TV talk shows, and she learned to understand and empathize with children's feelings. She developed skills and a little battery of tricks she practiced, and over time she became happier and more spiritual. She would never brag about it and say, 'Wow, I'm becoming more spiritual.' She just does it, just lives it, and she evolved into this extraordinary person—I really don't know anyone else like her—who is deep and inspirational and sets an example for us all."

According to Judy, Sandy has dealt with Jay's death the best of everyone in the family, principally by practicing her "distraction trick" of keeping herself busy—going out with friends, swimming every day for relaxation, attending lectures, taking care of her family. "Talking to her is immensely helpful to me," Judy says. "I talk to her every day and almost every night. In the beginning, when I was first dealing with my illness, I really leaned on her. She would say to me, 'You're going to get through this. It feels like the way you're feeling now is going to be forever, but it's not. It will change. Nothing in life is permanent.' I listen to everything she says, and I think about all the things she's told me when I'm flipping out."

Sandy's transformation from an uptight reactor to stressful events to a steadfastly optimistic survivor in the presence of tragedy followed a typical path: the desire to change, new ways of thinking and acting, and determined practice. She wanted to have a better relationship with her children than she had with her mother, and that started her off on her continuing quest to develop new habits of mind that contributed to her inner strength. "My big motto is, don't worry about things over which you have no control," she says. "Judy and I went to Overeaters Anonymous independently of each other and learned the Serenity Prayer: 'God grant me the serenity to accept the things I cannot change, the courage to change the things I can, and the wisdom to know the difference.' Of all the ideas I've come across, I don't think there's ever been a better key to dealing with life's obstacles than that."

Besides practicing positive mental habits, Sandy finds listening to uplifting music a big help in warding off depression.

"Marching music is my absolute favorite—I must have been an infantryman in my other life," she says. "After watching

"My big motto is, don't worry about things over which you have no control."

the Twin Towers go down again and again on TV, I was getting increasingly depressed. I took my tape player and walked up into the hills near my home and sat there, listening to my marching music, and it really gave me a lift."

Sandy gets the biggest lift nowadays watching the videotape of Judy's wedding. "Every time I want to be with Jay, I pop the tape into the VCR, and he steps right out of the screen," she says. "The wedding was unbelievable. Everyone was so elated that it was finally happening. It was Jay's shining moment to see his daughter get married. The expression on his face was so proud and happy—and so *relieved*, as my other children said at his funeral. Judy and Rick really made it special and their own. Rick came down the aisle to Dean Martin's "It's a Kick in the Head," very peppy and adorable, and everyone chuckled. Then the parents came down the aisle, and everything stopped. It got very quiet. A violin quartet began playing very somber music. We were all waiting for Judy, looking for her, and then all of a sudden the music switches to this wonderful, exuberant song—"I Feel Pretty"—and she starts down the aisle in her wedding gown, wearing a wig because she had just had her second summer round of chemotherapy, and I've never seen her so happy. Everyone stood up and clapped, and it was like she had a standing ovation. It was such a moment."

Judy's vows were refreshingly funny in some places ("It took me a long time to find you, and I think you and everyone here knows, I worked my ass off to do it!") and touching in others. Taking a page from David Letterman, she told Rick the ten reasons why she felt so lucky that he wanted to marry her. Her eighth one was, "I love that you go to every doctor's appointment with me and take such good care of me. And from the second we found out about the melanoma, you never left my side, and not once did you complain about being with someone dealing with cancer. That, to me, shows extraordinary strength of character. You have the most positive attitude of anyone I know (besides my mom). One of my vows is to emulate your positive fighting spirit when the going gets tough."

Rick used the word "miraculous" in his vows to describe his meeting Judy on an Internet dating service and the beautiful relationship that developed between the two of them and their families, including Rick's children from a previous marriage. He felt it was destiny that brought them together after waiting so long to find such happiness, and he quoted this passage from Rainer Maria Rilke's *Letters to a Young Poet:* "Destiny itself is like a wonderful wide tapestry in which every thread is guided by an unspeakably tender hand, placed beside another thread and held and carried by a hundred others." Speaking of their own "incredibly wide" tapestry developed in a relatively short span of a few years, Rick said, "I vow to you that I will continue to be there with you as we, and that unspeakably tender hand that guides the threads, weave it together over the years, no matter how difficult or complicated the pattern might become at times." Quoting another line—"I don't want reality—I want magic!"—from *A Streetcar Named Desire*, Rick revealed that for years his reality was something he wanted to escape from, but when Judy came into his life, she made his reality magical for the very first time. "And my vow to you," he said, "is to do whatever is in my power, for as long as I am on this earth, to make your reality as magical as you have made mine. You are a wonderful, beautiful, magical soul, Judy. . . . I love you, I'm honored to be your husband, and I vow to you that I will always live up to that honor."

Judy is thankful that her last memory of her father is seeing him alive and well and having him share her joy at her wedding. Although he was uncomfortable performing in public, he did a spirited dance with her to a song they sang privately together all the time, "I Want an Old-Fashioned Wedding" from *Annie Get Your Gun*. "The whole time he was begging me under his breath, 'All right, that's enough, please get me off, I can't stand this, let other people get up,'" Judy remembers, "but he was great."

There are other memories Judy has that will keep her father alive for her always—memories of how openly affectionate and adoring he was with her mother. "He would be in his thermal underwear or boxer shorts, dancing around in front of my mom in their bedroom, and I would be on the bed, watching him do these silly dances. My mom thought he was hilarious—I always enjoyed her being the best audience in the world—and sometimes he would grab her and kiss her, and she'd blush and say, 'Oh, stop it, Jay.' Another time we were at a fiftieth wedding anniversary party for some relatives, and I was hanging out with my dad at the table, and my mom was across the room, talking to some people. And my father said to me, 'Look at your mom. Isn't she beautiful? Is she gorgeous or what?' I just loved that."

There's another memory of her time alone with her father that Judy cherishes. "There's a night that's so clear in my head when my mom was away, and we went out to dinner, just the two of us, and were sitting at the bar," she says. "I was so depressed, just so down about my career. He asked if I wanted anything to drink, and I said no. I think I started to cry. And he said, 'Don't worry about it, kid. It's all going to work out.'

He wasn't usually so encouraging, but that night he was being so great and so supportive, and I'll never forget it."

Looking back on how she spent most of her twenties and thirties consumed with her career, Judy wonders why that was all she cared about for all those years. "Why was my self-worth all wrapped up in my career?" she asks. "That's why I ended up not being married until so much later. Now I think, who cares? It's just not as meaningful anymore." Judy makes it clear that she still cares about her work although not so obsessively, and she credits it for being a big factor in keeping her going because it takes her out of herself. "I love all the people there—my boss, my cowriters, the girls on the show—," she says, "and it's fun thinking about these imaginary lives on *Sex and the City* rather than mine. That and listening to my step-kids' problems—anything that keeps the focus off me—is a boon."

Judy has always been the kind of self-motivated person who tackles whatever is put in front of her with dispatch. "Any career decision I had to make, I just did it," she says. "After my dad died, I knew I had to come back to my home town and be with my mom, and I did it. Each time I come out of my surgeries, I have this intense drive to get back in life. It was easier in the beginning, but as time goes on I have a harder and harder time. I'm not as good as my mom is at not sitting around and thinking for big chunks of time. After a while it starts to sink in."

But Judy is finding the strength to go on. She feels exceptionally lucky to have Rick but isn't sure whether the destiny Rick spoke of in his wedding vows brought them together or whether it was just coincidence. "I'd love to think Rick's way," she says, "but then I think, why would I be dealing with cancer?" After a moment, she answers her own question. "It's not whether I'm going to get through this," she says, "but how." Having cancer has made Judy reorganize her priorities and accept her illness as a challenge. She realizes now that love is more important than anything else in life—the love lavished on her by

"It's not whether I'm going to get through this, but how."

Rick, her family, her many friends and colleagues, and the love that lives on in her memories of her father. She is grateful to have all that love, sustaining and indestructible, to see her through the toughest battle of her life. Ever her mother's daughter, she says, "I'm really blessed."

Postscript: On May 2, 2002, at the age of forty-four, Judy Toll lost her six-year battle with melanoma. She spent her last days scripting her own memorial service, mining her heartache for comic material until the very end and orchestrating her final show for the many fans who loved her.

The Best Remembrance

Grief turns into healing when you relinquish the pain and helplessness you feel, because there is nothing you can do to bring the deceased person back, and shift your thoughts to what you can do to honor that person's memory. *The best remembrance of a loved one is to carry on what that person stood for.* What unique qualities did that person possess? What were his or her interests or wishes? To insure that the meaning of that person's life continues after death, you can't dwell on your feelings of loss indefinitely. If you allow them to consume you, your focus becomes fixed on you—your rage, your sorrow, your loneliness—rather than on the person who is gone. Shift your focus to doing justice to that person's memory, and your pain will begin to diminish. Think of how the person who has died would want to be remembered and how you can preserve that person's impact. Let those thoughts be your guide.

If you're the survivor of a family member who has been murdered, the rage you feel is a particularly virulent emotion that can prevent you from honoring the memory of the person you lost. This emotion can also be self-destructive. Your rage is the same rage that drives people to commit murder. There is no comfort in it, and nothing good can come out of it. All it does is "feed off the soul until there is no soul left," as the nun in the gritty television prison drama *Oz* tells a frighteningly violent, bigoted inmate.

Although my daughter survived the car accident that left her severely brain-injured, the intense rage and hatred I initially felt toward the drunk driver only exacerbated my pain and would have rendered me dysfunctional had I not brought it under control. The same was true for Frank and Janet, the couple in this chapter whose nineteen-year-old daughter, Melissa, was raped and murdered while she was away at college. As long as they were overwhelmed by feelings of rage, a howling sense of injustice, and thoughts of revenge, they were inconsolable. But when they came into contact with other parents of murdered children who empathized with them and let them know they were not alone, they stopped tormenting themselves with futile anger and guilt and focused their energies on keeping Melissa's spirit alive.

Whether they are religious or personal, the customs, rituals, and ceremonies that help us maintain a connection with a loved one who has died are very healing. Many people light a candle on a holiday or on the anniversary of the person's death or give a gift in the name of the person. Some, like Sandy and Judy, watch family videos or reminisce; others, like Frank and Janet, keep a journal, or as Melissa's brother, Ryan, did on his graduation day, pay tribute to the person on special occasions. What we memorialize is not that the person died, but that the person lived. Parents who lost a baby in childbirth have the same need as anyone else to mourn their loss and commemorate the person who was born but didn't make it. One couple I know who lost an infant established a fund at the Philadelphia Zoo in his name. Another couple in my own family set up a scholarship at the University of Pennsylvania in the name of their son, who died shortly after he was born. Establishing a scholarship fund seems an especially apt way to memorialize young people.

One of the more heart-breaking aspects of the World Trade Center tragedy was the youth and bright promise of so many of the victims—talented, ambitious, optimistic young people who had come to New York City in pursuit of their

What we memorialize is not that the person died, but that the person lived.

dreams. Some of them were only a few years out of college when they died, and they had been in school for most of their lives. The friends of Johanna Sigmund, a twenty-six-year-old who was working at Fred Alger Management, Inc., when she was killed in the September 11th attacks, chose to honor her memory with a scholarship in her name to the school she loved, knowing that's what she would have wanted.

"Johanna and I went all through Springside School together from kindergarten through twelfth grade, and she felt that the school really helped to shape her personality and life," says Alexandra Morris, publicity and marketing manager at Doubleday at Random House and one of Johanna's closest friends. The Springside School is a small, private school in Chestnut Hill, Pennsylvania, where Johanna was a trivarsity athlete—playing award-winning field hockey, squash, and lacrosse—and earning four of the school's highest awards for drama, art, athletics, and leadership at her 1994 graduation.

After college, Alexandra and two other friends shared an apartment in New York with Johanna for almost four years until Alexandra got married. "Johanna had this old-fashioned, classic beauty that made people notice her whenever she walked into a room," says Alexandra, "and I've never met a person who didn't adore her. She was a wonderfully caring and giving person who made everyone around her feel good, because she had such a positive outlook on life and was so joyful and happy. She was like sunshine." But Johanna was more than just a smiley face. According to her friend, she contributed to many different people's lives and was always thinking of others and helping them. "There were homeless people who lived near us, and she'd bring them food," Alexandra remembers. "Once, she saw a girl fall as she was getting out of a cab and ran to help her. She had never seen the girl before, but she didn't mind getting the girl's blood all over herself. She went to the hospital with her, held her hand, stayed there with her the whole night, and made sure she was all right. She was just that kind of person. We knew that whatever we did to memorialize her, it would have to be something that combined her love of Springside School and helping someone in need."

It was Joseph Bonavita, Johanna's boyfriend, who came up with the idea of the scholarship in Johanna's name so that a promising student who otherwise couldn't afford a Springside education could experience all that it offered Johanna. Joe, whose dream was to be standing in church exchanging marriage vows with Johanna instead of delivering her eulogy, was devastated by her loss but determined to create something positive from it that would honor her legacy. With the full support of Johanna's parents, Joe and Alexandra collaborated on a letter that went out with a brochure to everyone they knew who might want to contribute to the scholarship fund. Drawn together by a survivors' bond, Johanna's boyfriend, her best friend, Johanna's brother John, Jr., and some other friends formed a committee to create an endowment through fund-raising activities and events. Joe, who works in investment banking at Lehman Brothers, hopes that the fund will eventually support six full scholarships for new recipients each year.

In his eulogy Joe recounted how Johanna's parents and her brother joined him to cheer her on as she ran in the New York Marathon in November of 2000. She was training to run in the Philadelphia Marathon the following November, but that goal was hijacked along with the planes that flew into the World Trade Center two months before. More than twenty relatives and friends participated in the marathon in her honor. In the midst of their sadness they came together to affirm life and finish something Johanna had started.

"One thing we all know is that Johanna would want for us to move forward, do something to help someone else, and enjoy life to the fullest the way she did," Alexandra says. Her friendship with Johanna was so deep and close that she sometimes has to stop herself from picking up the phone and calling Johanna when she has something she wants to share with her. "She was the truest type of friend," she says. "You could be completely yourself with her. If you wanted to confide in her about something, you would always know that she would never judge you or breathe a word about it to anyone." Like many others, Alexandra has found comfort in a journal and in her dreams. "Mostly I write about her, but I'll even write something to her sometimes, and it helps me sort out what I'm thinking," she says. "I've had a couple of dreams about her that make me feel connected to her in a certain sense." No matter what happens, Johanna will always be with her. "Even when I'm an old woman," Alexandra says, "I know there won't be a day when I don't think about her and the effect she had on my life—not just on mine, but on everyone who came into contact with her."

Both Alexandra and Joe have found solace in their religious faith, but their greatest source of strength and inspiration is Johanna herself. "I know this isn't the last time I may lose someone this important to me," Alexandra says, "but you can't keep obsessing about what's going to happen after this. You just have to realize it's part of life and get into this mode, whether it's religious or not, of having faith. I really believe Johanna is at peace and in a better place. I keep asking how she would handle the situation I'm in now, and I know she would want to make the best of it in some way. I try to be like her and emulate her outlook of enjoying life and making the most of everything."

Joe turned to a priest, a family friend, "because I needed a re-affirmation of my own faith, faith in religion, faith in humanity, just plain old faith in life." One of the priest's views on life turned out to be a particularly appropriate one for dealing with the loss of Johanna. "He said life is like a marathon," Joe relates, "a grueling journey, a test of our will and our resolve to continue on and strive through all the pain and all the hurt and the challenges of life." Facing the hardest part of his marathon at Johanna's memorial service, Joe told the mourners: "I know that Johanna is with me, on the sideline, cheering me on, urging me to finish, telling me to never give up." With hope for the future, Joe will continue his race to provide a young girl with financial need the chance to have a quality education and honor the life and memory of the woman he lost but will always love.

Unfortunately, it often takes the loss of a loved one earlier than expected to make us fully comprehend the impermanence of everything in the physical world. Change is programmed into every facet of our existence from moment to moment. The pain of loss becomes more bearable if we keep the reality of this impermanence in mind, both by not expecting to be spared the pain of loss and by not expecting the intensity of our pain to last forever. The concept of whatever we have being on loan to us makes it easier to accept having it taken away and also relieves us of the unbearable feeling that our suffering will never subside. The surest way to make our suffering subside is to place a higher value on the impact that our loved one had on us than we place on the person's loss.

More than the length or brevity of our days on earth, love is our ultimate legacy. Love is all that matters, and love never leaves.

Strength-Building Exercise:
"Letting Go and Holding On"

This exercise shows you how to maintain a healthy connection with a loved one who has died and find ways to lessen your feelings of anger, sorrow, and helplessness. By following these steps you can hasten your return to emotional stability and find some kind of benefit from your loss—new insights into yourself, a new role, deepened spirituality based on understanding the realities of human existence, the power of a positive outlook, greater appreciation for life. A survivor can't take a passive response to loss; you must respond creatively with an attitude and actions that make the spirit of your loved one a motivating force for achieving happiness again. Here are some recommendations:

- Write letters to your loved one or log onto memorial sites on the Internet where you can leave messages.
- Keep a journal marking milestones and including photos and other mementoes of the deceased person.
- Develop remembrance rituals.
- Keep symbolic representations of your loved one—letters, personal effects, drawings.
- Tell stories about the person.
- Communicate with the person in meditation, mental or verbal conversations, and gravesite visits.
- Study what your dreams are telling you about your connections with your loved one.
- Join a support group (use a search engine like AOL or Yahoo to find one).
- Engage in activities to reduce pain, anxiety, and sadness (physical activity, art therapy, a hobby, volunteer work, a class, listening to music, etc.).
- Cultivate an optimistic outlook and the art of positive thinking on a daily basis. Practice becoming aware of all you can appreciate and enjoy through each of your five senses, concentrating on one a day; repeatedly practice shifting your thoughts from what you have lost to what you still have.
- Resolve to honor your loved one by living the rest of your life in the most productive way possible.

10

From Grief to Grace

If you're committed to following the three fundamental principles in this book—*embracing misfortune as an opportunity for transformation, reframing loss as possibility,* and *letting go of who you were in order to become more of who you are*—this last leg of your journey toward resilience will culminate in a renewal of your spirit. Having transformed yourself from a passive victim into a creative survivor, you can now set about to transform yourself from a survivor into a healer, either as an inspiring example for others or as a promoter of positive change. I call this a state of grace, not in any religious sense, but meaning simply that you feel life is good and *you* are good regardless of your circumstances. You have the profound and sustainable inner strength that only persevering through life's struggles can bring. You also have the unconditional happiness that comes from always finding something to be grateful for and rejoice in even though life isn't perfect.

As a resourceful, independent person, in touch with your inner strength and willing to take risks, you can be sure that the intense emotions caused by your grief will find an outlet in productivity. Whether it's in artistic expression, business, science, the political arena, social activism, or in your relationships with family and friends, you will impart meaning to your loss by creating something new that adds beauty or enjoyment to the world or improves the lives of others in some way. If you now take the skills you've been taught—acceptance of hardship for your

The gift we ultimately find through loss is the heart and soul of ourselves.

own growth, the ability to see things in a new light, positive thinking— and use them to transform your pain into empowerment, you will never feel powerless again. The gift we ultimately find through loss is the heart and soul of ourselves.

A Good Feeling

Of all the benefits that make a misfortune a "blessing in disguise," connecting with a purpose larger than yourself can be the most far-reaching. Transforming your private pain into the power to help others is one of the deepest sources of fulfillment that your encounter with adversity can bring. Nothing gives more meaning to the heartache you've experienced than turning it into a redemptive force.

When I founded Wives Self Help on an impulse to connect with other women who were experiencing the same anguish I was over the breakup of my marriage, I had no idea how beneficial helping others would be to my own spirits. For one thing, I came into contact with victims of domestic violence and other forms of abuse whose problems made mine seem minor in comparison. More importantly, I also discovered that offering assistance to the hotline callers gave me a visceral feeling of gratification deep inside. Each time I hung up the hotline phone knowing that I'd made another person's pain a little less overwhelming, I felt my own pain that much less. As

"Joan," the pseudonym I'd given myself for the sake of anonymity, I became a happier person than I'd been as myself.

Loss becomes redemptive when it takes us out of ourselves, out of the bell jar that magnifies and intensifies our sorrows, and unites us with all other human beings. Empathy is programmed into us because we are social beings who are dependent on each other for survival. Studies have shown that acting empathetically is not only emotionally and spiritually rewarding but is actually good for our health. When we help others, our bodies respond with an immediate biochemical boost to our immune system. The good feeling we get whenever we channel our grief into concern for others and show kindness to another in pain is the signal our bodies give us that we're doing the right thing.

Many people who've lost loved ones in a traumatic way have found an outlet for their feelings of helplessness, anger, and grief by getting involved in a cause for positive change. Some who had never been activists before felt impelled to start groups that are having a significant impact on our political and social systems. This is not a path for everyone to take, and I don't mean to say that those who take it are better or stronger than anyone else. But if you feel inclined to pursue this path, or even if you don't, the next three personal stories are encouraging and instructive. They show that you can start out at the grassroots level in any kind of venture with not much more than your own passion, conviction, and some good friends who want to help, and extraordinary things can happen.

> **Loss becomes redemptive when it takes us out of ourselves and unites us with all other human beings.**

Marian Fontana, who started the 9/11 Widows' and Victims' Families Association in the kitchen of her Brooklyn

apartment, is an example of how empowered we can become when we channel our grief into political action in
memory of a loved one.

A Moral Force: Marian Fontana

It was the day of their eighth wedding anniversary.
Firefighter Dave Fontana came off the night shift at
Brooklyn's Squad 1, a special operation command unit, and
called his wife, Marian, to tell her to meet him at 9:00 so
they could go into Manhattan and spend the day together
celebrating. A sculptor before he turned firefighter, Dave
planned for them to take a tour of the sculpture collection at
the Whitney museum, and Marian made a reservation at a
restaurant in Central Park. She was waiting for him on
Seventh Avenue, where he was supposed to pick her up, but
he never got there. Minutes after he phoned her, a five alarm
call sounded, and Dave, never one to miss a fire, jumped on
the rig and took off to answer the call. He was one of twelve
firefighters from his squad who died trying to rescue people
when the Twin Towers collapsed in flames. At thirty-seven,
he left behind the two people who mattered to him more
than anything in the world, Marian, his thirty-five-year-old
wife who fell in love with him in college, and his five-year-
old son, Aiden, whose name in Irish means "little fire."

Three weeks later, when Marian was still deep in grief and
hadn't even cleaned out Dave's locker, she got word that the
fire department was going to shut down her husband's firehouse and relocate the remaining men to Manhattan to fill the
spots vacated by the disaster. "I was enraged to hear that,"
Marian says. "I'm the only fire wife who lives in the neighborhood, and I spent a lot of time at the firehouse with the guys. I
guess my anger kind of started me on this mission."

Her mission was to become a spokesperson for the 9/11 firefighter widows and other family members who felt that city officials were ignoring them and dishonoring the memory of their loved ones. A writer and performer of one-woman shows, Marian is a warm, honest, sensitive, and unassuming person who had always funneled her drive and talent into the creative life rather than politics. Although not inflammatory, she is passionate about her opinions and drew the courage to stand up for them out of her desire to honor her husband's memory.

It was late Sunday night when she heard that the firehouse would be closed down by Tuesday at 9:00 AM, and she sprang into action. "I called a few friends in my neighborhood, and they were very support-

"I guess my anger kind of started me on this mission."

ive," she says. "I stayed up all night writing fliers to post around the neighborhood for a rally. By the time I took my son to school Monday morning, my friends had already plastered the neighborhood with posters, and there were mobs of people with petitions in front of the school and at the firehouse. By 4:00 in the afternoon, we had every news crew and every politician there."

Marian and the supporters she mobilized into a small army won the battle. Faced with such fervent opposition, the fire department officials backed down from their plan. "We managed to keep the firehouse open," she says, "and the guys together."

The next battle arose when eighteen of the several hundred off-duty firefighters protesting the cutback in the number of firefighters in the debris-removal and retrieval operation at Ground Zero were arrested after scuffling with police officers at the site. "I knew the guys were doing the rally, so

I called some media people I'm friendly with to go down there and cover it," Marian says. "By the time it hit the news, the firefighters were being portrayed as violent. I found out from my reporter friends that other media people were blowing a calm, quiet march and protest out of proportion. They said, 'You have to do something.'"

Marian called Lynne Tierney, the deputy fire commissioner for intergovernmental affairs, and told her, "A lot of families, including myself, are very upset about the cutbacks, and we're getting no communication from the department. There's a lot of rumbling, and this lack of communication is going to blow up in your face. Maybe you guys want to try to address it before it bubbles over." Tierney said, "I'll get the mayor and the commissioner to meet with you."

Marian brought a couple of other widows with her to the informal meeting held in someone's apartment. "Mayor Giuliani was very receptive," she says. "He said he would drop the charges against all but one of the firemen who were arrested and that he would add the manpower. One of the things I really wanted was to continue a dialogue with the mayor, and he agreed to that. So we continued to have weekly meetings with him and address concerns as they came up."

Out of that first meeting with Mayor Rudolph W. Giuliani, the 9/11 Widows' and Victims' Families Association was born. With Marian as its president and a database of some six hundred people, the nonprofit organization has become the voice of the grieving fire families, tackling such issues as restrictions on the money families can receive under the Victims' Compensation Bill. "I don't really care if I get any money," Marian says. "My immediate expenses were met by charitable donations, for which I'm very grateful, and my husband's pension is livable. It's just a matter of not wanting the middle-of-the-road guy, the blue-collar guy, to get short-changed. It seems wrong." Giuliani's successor, Mayor Michael R. Bloomberg, came to the group's rally on this funding issue and spoke to the three hundred people assembled there. The group is also holding forums with artists, architects, and others to make sure that the disaster site, which they consider to be a burial ground, will fittingly memorialize their loved ones.

Credited by *The New York Times* for lending a "moral force" to the formative argument for restoring a larger presence of firefighters at Ground Zero, Marian takes a more humble and pragmatic view of what she has accomplished. "I certainly wouldn't pat myself on the back," she says. "On some level I was redirecting my anger and grief into a good cause, and on another level it was just a distraction from feeling the sadness and sitting in my apartment without my husband, with too much to bear. So keeping myself busy and getting out into the world and helping the other families who were all going through the same thing was a way of distracting myself from my own pain. And it wasn't like I had a choice. I felt propelled by my husband and what he would have wanted."

"It wasn't like I had a choice. I felt propelled by my husband and what he would have wanted."

Dave Fontana—a big, muscular guy with a square jaw and rugged good looks—had his feet planted in two worlds. One was the vigorous world of a firefighter and outdoorsman who loved to build things; go hiking, kayaking, and mountain-climbing; and test himself to the limit physically. The other was the artistic and intellectual world of a sculptor, historian, and student of yoga. The nephew of a soldier killed in the Battle of the Bulge, he spent two years researching the New York City firefighters who died in combat during World War II. Six months before his own death, Dave organized a firehouse ceremony to honor two South Brooklyn firefighters who lost their lives fighting the Nazis. But all of that was secondary to how much Dave cared for his family. "His main focus in life was on myself and our son," Marian says. "He was very devoted. His idea of a good night was hanging out with his family."

Although Dave's body wasn't recovered until December, Marian held the memorial service for him in October on his birthday and delivered a beautiful eulogy that paid tribute to the remarkable man he was. In it she said, "Even though I am a firefighter's wife, I never really imagined losing Dave. He seemed as impossible to bring down, as solid, strong, and indomitable as the Towers seemed to be. . . . Falling in love with Dave was like taking a long, reflective walk on the beach and then finding that perfect shell or stone. His gentle nature, genuine sweetness, outrageous humor, loving soul, and creative spirit won me over. The more I got to know Dave, the more walks we took, the more deeply I fell in love with him, and in our seventeen years together I fell in love with him over and over again. . . . I knew he would be a good dad, but he embraced fatherhood with a zeal that surpassed my wildest expectations. . . . I remember one night when Aidan was tiny and refused to fall asleep. After hours he finally nodded off, and I tiptoed out of the room. A few minutes later, I caught Dave sneaking into Aidan's room to make sure he was covered up with his blanket. I scolded Dave, fearful that he would wake him up. A little while later, I heard Dave in Aidan's room again. I was furious. I threw open the door to find Dave leaning over the crib whispering 'I love you' gently in Aidan's ear over and over. He stood up, dimples folded in a wide smile, and said, 'I just want Aidan to know, deep in his consciousness, how much I really love him.'"

By doing from her heart what she feels Dave would have wanted her to do, Marian is finding the good to come out of losing the love of her life. She is whispering in his ear how much she really loves him.

* * *

Channeling your anger and grief over the loss of a loved one into a movement for political or social action is, as Marian found, so powerful a choice from the heart that it feels like no choice at all. It's not the kind of deliberate decision you arrive at after sitting down and weighing all the pros and cons but rather an irresistible creative urge to give life to the essence of the person who has vanished. When the person died because of some shocking injustice, the urge to right the wrong and spare others the same fate is a call to action that stirs a responsive chord in almost everyone who hears it.

Righting a Wrong: Boaz Keysar and Linda Ginzel

Boaz Keysar, a psychology professor at the University of Chicago, was at home on May 12, 1998, when he got the phone call every parent dreads. His wife, Linda Ginzel, who teaches managerial psychology at the same university, was still at work. The caller told Boaz to go to the hospital across the street from the couple's home. Their sixteen-month-old son, Danny, had been taken there after being badly hurt in an accident at his day-care center in a private home. Linda was alarmed to see police cars outside the center as she stopped on her way home from work to pick Danny up. With growing apprehension, she was escorted to the hospital. By the time either one of the parents arrived at the hospital, Danny was dead.

It appeared to be an accident that could not have been prevented. Danny awoke from a nap in a portable crib called the Playskool Travel-Lite, stood up in the crib and was leaning on a top side-rail when the locking mechanism failed. The rail collapsed, catching the toddler's neck in a V and strangling him as his body weight dragged him down.

"We thought it was a freak accident, a one-time occurrence in millions of events," Linda says. "Danny happened to be the victim, and there was nothing to be done." The day after Danny's funeral, a friend of the couple showed them an article in the *Chicago Tribune* that completely transformed the way they thought about Danny's death. The article said Danny was the fifth child to die in this crib and that the crib had been recalled five years before. The grieving parents were stunned. "Not only was Danny the fifth kid to die," Boaz says, "but according to the article, only 12,000 units of the crib had been sold. The ratio of deaths to the number of cribs was frightening. Suddenly we realized this wasn't an accident; it was a systematic thing."

Boaz and Linda, who went to school in Princeton and taught at Stanford, have friends from all over the country, and many came to be with them while they were mourning. Linda says, "We were all sitting there, trying to understand, how could it be that a recalled product was in use in a licensed day-care center that had been inspected eight days before Danny's death? What did it mean to be recalled? How come it was recalled, but nobody knew? Why didn't the state know? Why didn't the day-care provider know? Why didn't we know? Our business is information. We had a hard time accepting the status quo."

Instead of getting stuck in their own pain, the couple shifted their attention to alerting other potential victims. Besides Kolcraft, the manufacturer of Travel-Lite, four other companies made similar portable cribs with top rails that could collapse because of unsafe locking mechanisms. "The first thing we did was to send an e-mail warning to thousands of people, who forwarded it to thousands more around the world," Boaz says. "It was a very compelling message," Linda adds, "so it proliferated very quickly. We got hundreds of e-mails back, and some of them said, 'Thank you for your message. I pulled my sleeping child from one of these recalled cribs.'"

It disturbed Boaz and Linda to know how many unsafe children's products were out there that nobody knew about and how ineffective recalls are. That was the impetus for them to start Kids in Danger, a nonprofit organization to promote the development of safer children's products, advocate for laws governing children's product safety, and educate the public about dangerous children's products. "We started funding it with our savings," Boaz says, "and friends came through with donations. A colleague of ours from the university designed our first Web site and put it up within a week. We started getting grants, and now we have an executive director, two fulltime staff and an office in downtown Chicago, and people doing work for Kids in Danger all over the country." Linda adds, "People are shocked to learn that children's products are not required to be tested before they're sold. They can't believe how Danny died and that he's not an isolated victim. Once people know the truth, they feel compelled to act."

Through what they call "an amazing community effort," the couple's Kids in Danger has

> "Once people know the truth, they feel compelled to act."

gotten federal legislation introduced to require the testing of children's products. State legislation, enacted in Illinois, is pending in five other states, barring the sale of recalled products and requiring state licensing agencies to check for them in day-care centers. On a personal level, Boaz and Linda, who have had another son since Danny's death, feel their lives have been changed forever. "We do what we can to beat the drum," Linda says. As teachers, they are using Danny's story as a case study at Harvard's business school and other business schools around the country. "We're trying to reach managers and future managers," Linda says, "and make them think about their decisions and the kinds of tradeoffs they make every day."

Hoping to attack the root cause of the problem that killed their son—the way children's products are designed, tested, and marketed—Boaz and Linda sued Kolcraft, the manufacturer of the crib, and Hasbro, the company that affixed its respected Playskool brand to the crib without ever testing it. The companies wanted to settle out of court but insisted on the gag order that companies customarily demand in settlements of lawsuits by consumers over products. Boaz and Linda turned them down flat. "We wanted to go to trial," Linda says. "We wanted the public to have the information. We felt that if companies hadn't forced parents to sign confidentiality statements earlier and this information had gotten out, then maybe our son would be alive."

Boaz and Linda stuck it out to the very end. Moments before jury selection, Kolcraft and Hasbro agreed to pay the couple three million dollars in damages and not to bar them from speaking out about the lawsuit and what led up to it. "The amount was unprecedented for this kind of case," Boaz says, "because an infant's life is basically not worth very much economically in the legal system. Children don't have an income, and they're considered a liability because you have to feed, clothe, and educate them. When they deposed us, the companies' lawyers argued that since we didn't expect Danny to support us, his death didn't cost us any-thing—in fact, he saved us money because we didn't have to raise him. At the end, after we told them we had no out-standing bills from Danny's death, they asked, 'So what do you want from us?' Linda answered, 'My son is dead.'

"Litigation pressure is not going to make the industry behave more responsibly," Linda says, "but I think every case should be litigated, because every data point that is out in public will contribute to the trend across time. There has to be an organized political movement, and we really believe that the next big consumer movement is going to be in chil-dren's products. You watch us make it happen."

Boaz says, "Every time we hear from somebody who was touched by this, we feel that it's Danny who is giving life to kids we're saving. We didn't make a conscious deci-sion that we were going to change this problem or change the world; we just knew we had to do it."

"Kids in Danger is Danny's legacy," Linda says, her voice breaking as she goes on: "He didn't have an opportu-nity to create his own legacy, but we're doing this in his honor. He should not have died this way, and neither should any other child."

> **"We feel that it's Danny who is giving life to kids we're saving."**

* * *

For people like Boaz Keysar and Linda Ginzel and Marian Fontana, there is an instinctive feeling almost from the outset that their mission is something they have to do to honor their loved one's memory. But there are others who find their way into their missions seemingly by accident—a "meaningful co-incidence," as it turns out.

A Remarkable Journey: Deborah Spungen

Nancy Spungen was twenty years old when she was murdered by her rock star boyfriend, Sid Vicious, with whom she'd been living in New York for a year and a half. It was 1978, the height of the sex, drugs, and rock-and-roll era, and the murder made all the headlines. Sid Vicious was arrested and charged with the murder, but he died of a drug overdose while he was out on bail awaiting trial. Nancy was murdered in October, and by February the case was closed.

"In those days there wasn't much being done as far as not blaming the victim," Nancy's mother, Deborah Spungen, says, "so Nancy was blamed and vilified by all kinds of media." The fact is, Nancy was mentally ill. "She had been treated for emotional problems since she was two," Deborah says, "and was hospitalized many times from the age of ten on. There weren't hospitals or beds then that were specifically for children, so if anything, those interventions did more harm than good." The Spungens didn't get most of their daughter's diagnoses until after her death. "One treatment facility made a diagnosis of schizophrenia," Deborah says, "but they didn't share that with us until I found out about it afterwards when I got her records. Other people who diagnosed her in hindsight thought she had some kind of psychosis or maybe manic-depression. There was no question that she had some serious problems, but no one really knew what they were or what to do about them."

Deborah thinks the thing that confused the issue was that Nancy was so intelligent—people thought she could handle more than she could. "The school for emotionally disturbed children she went to recommended that she go to college at the age of sixteen," she says. "She went to the University of Colorado, got into trouble there, and was back home in Philadelphia a year later." Nancy stayed in Philadelphia for a while, got more and more out of control, and left for the rock music scene in New York. "She always had this fascination with cutting-edge music," Deborah says. "If she liked a group, you could be sure they were going to be a hit the next year. Maybe if her head had been on straight, she could have been successful in the music business."

Even though they had a feeling that Nancy was on a collision course with violence and drugs, Deborah and her husband never anticipated that their troubled daughter would end up murdered. "We thought of suicide," she says, "which was definitely an issue with her after numerous attempts, and we thought about a drug overdose, but we didn't think about murder. It's the sudden violence of it at the hands of another person that really sets it apart. It's so traumatic to have someone die that way. The trauma is the dominant feature as opposed to just the grief, but there wasn't a recognition of that at the time. The responses we got from professionals and other people were not appropriate because they didn't understand the full spectrum of the experience."

Some couples are torn apart by a child's death, but Nancy's murder cemented the relationship between Deborah and her husband even more. "There was so much incredible stress during Nancy's life, and then that part was over," Deborah says, "and we found it easier, at least on the issue of what happened to her, to function as a unit. We were very fortunate that our friends and family were very supportive of us in every way, and were really very nonjudgmental."

Deborah was forty-one when Nancy died and had been too busy in the 1960s and 1970s taking care of a home and raising Nancy and her younger brother and sister to do much else. Working in a health food store, and later in the computer end of direct mail marketing, comprised her whole job history up to that point. She certainly had no intention of becoming an advocate and caregiver for the families of homicide victims until she herself entered into that company. Taking on that role was a "spontaneous" thing—a synchronous event, one might say—that she happened into two years after Nancy was murdered.

"A lot of people say, almost from the beginning, I've got to do something, I've got to change this, other people shouldn't have to go through this," she says, "but for me, it wasn't like that. I had time to process what happened, and then someone asked me to appear on a local TV show with people from a group called Parents of Murdered Children, which was out of Cincinnati and had only a few chapters at that time. I had seen them on TV once before and called because I wanted to go to a local chapter for help—I didn't want to start one—but they didn't have a chapter in Philadelphia. I talked to them for a while, and they said they were coming into town in about six months to be on TV and asked if I wanted to be on the show and represent the Philadelphia chapter. For some unknown reason, I said yes. Once I said it, that was it. People started to call after the show. Then we had the first support group meeting at our home and became the sixth chapter in the United States."

The next step came a few months later when the former mayor of Philadelphia, Edward Rendell, who was then district attorney, came to one of their meetings. He set a course of action for Deborah to follow—accompanying family members of homicide victims to court. The more involved she became in victim advocacy, the more she wanted to do. With a small grant from the Philadelphia district attorney's office, she set up the Anti-Violence Partnership of Philadelphia. It was the first victim advocate organization in the United States that was specifically developed and designed for the "covictims" of homicide.

"I coined the word *covictim* because it is the family member who stands in for the victim in every way," Deborah says. That name, along with *traumatic grief*, another term coined by Deborah, has since passed into everyday language. "There was a victims' movement in the early 1980s," she says, "but nobody recognized the covictims of homicide or acknowledged them. They often called them 'significant others,' but prosecutors around the country didn't invite them to be involved. Nobody told them what was going on. They'd go to a hearing—if they even heard about it—and half the time nobody told them it had been postponed. I started to realize that there were people who needed to be educated and empowered and also needed someone who could walk with them in their pain. I felt that being their voice for a while and walking with them on their journey was something I needed to do."

It wasn't just the covictims who needed to be educated; bureaucrats also had much to learn. Deborah became what she calls "a flea on the back of a dog." She annoyed enough people in the criminal justice system that they began to be sensitive to the needs of covictims and treat them equally with other victims of violent crime. Although there was a lot she knew intuitively from her own experience, she felt there was more she needed to learn, so she went back to school. Because she continued to work, she completed a dual master's program in law and social policy over three years instead of two.

> "I felt that being their voice for a while and walking with them on their journey was something I needed to do."

Her work in court was time-consuming and physically tiring and had her running from one courtroom to another and yet another in one day. In addition to accompanying covictims to court and sitting with them, she helped them fill out forms for death benefits and reimbursement for funeral expenses. Prosecutors and the police routinely began referring victims' families to her agency for assistance. "After a while it was second nature that the family was always included in things," Deborah says, "and that we were always there with them."

As Deborah's agency grew, it became a model for other organizations throughout the country. She put together a curriculum and received a grant from the United States Department of Justice's Office for Victims of Crime to go to different cities and train sixty people at a time—social workers, victim advocates, trauma doctors and nurses, police, all kinds of caregivers—on how to deal with covictims of homicides. What was once mostly a small, grassroots operation has become institutionalized. "I find it very gratifying that most prosecutors' offices and most police departments now have their own advocates working just with the families of homicide victims," Deborah says. "When I started, there were maybe 300 victims' agencies in the country, and now there are 10,000."

Several years after Nancy's death, Deborah began writing a book about Nancy's life. "I thought there were a lot of other Nancies out there, either mentally ill, as she was, or emotionally disturbed or who also had been murdered," she says. "I wanted people to know they weren't alone." Called *And I Don't Want to Live This Life*, the book was published in 1983 and has since sold about 350,000 copies in paperback alone.

In the beginning, Deborah looked upon taking her pain, anger, and grief and turning it into some kind of activity or action that would help others as her eulogy for Nancy. She wanted to cast a laudatory light on her maligned daughter's brief, tragic life through action rather than words. "I really did think of what I was doing as a eulogy for Nancy, because she was certainly the impetus for everything," she says. "But after a eulogy gets written, that's the end of it. At some point you put your own experience behind you, and the work stands on its own. You do it for other people, and you definitely get more back than you give."

Deborah was honored at the White House by President Clinton and by Janet Reno. "I received the honor, but I felt it wasn't just for me," she says. "It was for all the covictims who are now recognized and acknowledged and are not ignored any more." Going from Nancy's murder to running support groups to working in court in a pioneering way to taking victim advocacy to a level far broader and more structured than before has been a remarkable journey for Deborah. She has learned that you can't ever go back to normal again—you go forward and get to normal in a new way. "You get to a new normal," she says. "In any relationship that ends, whether it's by death or something else,

> You can't ever go back to normal again—you go forward and get to normal in a new way.

you can't fix it, and you can't make it better. You integrate the loss into your life and restructure your life with that experience as part of it. You really are the same person as before, but you're changed in many ways." In short, you've let go of who you were and have become more of who you are.

The Artist in You

The three examples I've given of people who regenerated themselves after the worst kind of loss—the traumatic death of a loved one—show how creative and powerful we can become when we channel our anger and grief into positive action. But not everyone is inclined to start or become active in a political or social movement in response to suffering a loss. Some of us, and you may be one of them, may find an outlet for our pain in artistic expression.

Like social activism, artistic expression actually has a physiological basis for making us feel better: It acts as a therapeutic release for the sadness that might otherwise become damaging to our health. Researchers into the link between loss and achievement believe that the pressure of intense sadness actually triggers a chemical reaction in the brain that generates a surge of creativity. Taking flight from painful feelings into the realm of fantasy and imagination helps many people cope better with stress at the same time that they are creating works of value. Throughout history, writers, artists, and musicians have channeled the pain of personal loss or of some hardship they've experienced into lasting works of beauty, power, and insight that have touched the souls of millions of others.

You, too, can find an outlet for your anger and sadness and a symbolic way to restore what you've lost in the words you write, the paintings you draw, the crafts you create, or the music you compose or play. Even if it's only on a small scale or for your own private benefit, you can use whatever talent you have to perpetuate your connection with a loved one who has died or to convert the pain of loss into a new reason to go on living.

Lou Weiss, of Tamarac, Florida, averted the fate of losing the will to live by taking up playing the violin at the age of ninety-two when he lost his wife of fifty-two years to cancer. I never met Weiss, but I was impressed when I read about him in the *Sun Sentinel*. A lifelong musician, he had never played the violin and was discouraged from learning to play it by a violin teacher who told him he was too old to learn a decade before. His sons, fearful that their dad would not recover from the enormous loss of his long-time spouse, bought him a violin for his ninety-second birthday. Undeterred by failing eyesight and arthritis in his right hand, Weiss began playing the violin every day and found a way to validate his life rather than shrink away from it. His renewed zest for living encouraged him to do many things he'd never done before, including preparing all his meals and doing his laundry. At his ninety-third birthday celebration, Weiss gave a concert for his family. Skillfully moving his bow across the violin they'd given him—a gift that made him glad he was still alive—he played *God Bless America*.

Strength-Building Exercise:
"Connecting with a Larger Purpose"

Think of any activity, on a small scale or large, that might be a productive outlet for your feelings of anger or sorrow. These are some questions to ask yourself that can steer you toward a fruitful and fulfilling larger purpose:

- What have I learned from this experience that I can share with others in a similar situation to help them cope?
- How can I prevent others from having to go through what I did?
- Should I join an existing organization or start one of my own?
- Can I express the passions stirred up by what I've gone through in word, music, or art?
- What message is there that I want to impart to others and what is the form of expression most appropriate for me?

- What can I do and how can I live my life to make something positive come out of this experience?

Take advantage of the enormous transformative power in life's disappointments, crises, and tragedies and use it to recreate yourself, your relationship with others, or your dreams. Harness that power to a new purpose—one truer to or larger than yourself—and you will find a deeper, more meaningful level of fulfillment than you have ever known.

Conclusion

Resilient people are no more gifted than anyone else—they simply know how to use the gift of creativity, which we all have. We are all artists in a sense, writers of our own life story, painters of our own portrait, composers of our own signature song. Pain and struggle are a natural part of the creative process, but we can regenerate ourselves in some way from whatever challenges, great or small, life hands us. The death of a loved one can motivate us to make our own lives more meaningful; an illness can make us appreciate life more and draw closer to the people we love; the loss of a job can put us in touch with talents waiting to be developed or dreams too long deferred; the breakup of a relationship can give us a new perspective on being a loving person or can impel us to take a whole new direction in life; a disabling accident can teach us how to adapt to change resourcefully and still make our own unique contributions to the world.

We all wish we could accomplish this growth and regeneration without an event that if someone told us in advance we'd have to go through, we'd say, "No way. I'd never be able to do it." But we're more resilient than we think. Our hardships are the means by which we can transcend the thoughts that limit us and reach a higher, more empowering consciousness and a more loving relationship with ourselves and others. We can all get through whatever challenges are thrown at us, aiming for grace and achieving it, as long as we accept each struggle as an opportunity for transformation, see the possibilities in loss, move forward toward our choices from the heart with a new sense of purpose, and have caring and compassionate people to accompany us on our journey. And that's what our journey is all about—our struggles and persevering through them and finding out how strong we really are.

Bibliography

Berg, Rav. *Secret Codes of the Universe*. The Kabbalah Centre, New York, New York, 2000.

Bernstein, Judith R. *When the Bough Breaks: Forever After the Death of a Son or Daughter*. Andrews McMeel Publishing, Kansas City, Missouri, 1998.

Bolen, Jean Shinoda. *Life-Threatening Illness and the Search for Meaning*. Simon and Schuster, New York, New York, 1998.

Bolles, Richard Nelson. *What Color Is Your Parachute? 2001: A Practical Manual for Job-Hunters and Career-Changers*. Ten Speed Press, Berkeley, California, 2001.

Bridges, William. *Transitions: Making Sense of Life's Changes*. Perseus Books, Cambridge, Massachusetts, 1980.

———. *The Way of Transition: Embracing Life's Most Difficult Moments*. Perseus Books, Cambridge, Massachusetts, 2000.

Cameron, Julia. *The Artist's Way: A Spiritual Path to Higher Creativity*. Jeremy P. Tarcher/Putnam, New York, New York, 1992.

Chodron, Pima. *The Wisdom of No Escape and the Path of Loving-Kindness*. Shambhala, Boston, Massachusetts, 1991.

Chopra, Deepak. *How to Know God: The Soul's Journey into the Mystery of Mysteries*. Crown Publishing Group, New York, New York, 2001.

Cohen, Marion Deutsche. *Dirty Details: The Days and Nights of a Well Spouse*. Temple University Press, Philadelphia, Pennsylvania, 1996.

Csikszentmihalyi, Mihaly. *Creativity: Flow and the Psychology of Discovery and Invention*. HarperPerennial, New York, New York, 1997.

The Dalai Lama and Cutler, Howard C. *The Art of Happiness: A Handbook for Living*. Riverhead Books/Penguin Putnam, New York, New York, 1998.

Gafni, Marc. *Soul Prints: Your Path to Fulfillment*. Pocket Books/Simon and Schuster, New York, New York, 2001.

Gawain, Shakti. *Creative Visualization*. New World Library, 14 Pamaron Way, Novato, California, 1995.

Goleman, Daniel. *Emotional Intelligence*. Bantam Books, New York, New York, 1995.

Hopcke, Robert H. *There Are No Accidents: Synchronicity and the Stories of Our Lives*. Riverhead Books/Penguin Putnam, New York, New York, 1998.

Jamison, Kay Redfield. *Night Falls Fast: Understanding Suicide*. Random House, New York, New York, 2000.

Kushner, Harold S. *When Bad Things Happen to Good People*, Avon Books, New York, New York, 1983.

Lord, Janice Harris. *No Time for Goodbyes: Coping with Sorrow, Anger, and Injustice After a Tragic Death*. Pathfinder Publishing of California, Oxnard, California, 2000.

Mace, Nancy L., and Rabins, Peter V. *36-Hour Day: A Family Guide to Caring for Persons with Alzheimer Disease, Related Dementing Illnesses, and Memory Loss in Later Life*. Warner, New York, New York, 2001.

Maxwell, John C. *Failing Forward: Turning Mistakes Into Stepping Stones for Success*. Thomas Nelson, Nashville, Tennessee, 2001.

Myss, Caroline. *Anatomy of the Spirit: The Seven Stages of Power and Healing*. Three Rivers Press/Crown Publishers, New York, New York, 1996.

———. *Sacred Contracts: Awakening Your Divine Potential*. Random House Value Publishing, New York, New York, 2002.

Noel, Brook, and Blair, Pamela D. *I Wasn't Ready to Say Goodbye: Surviving, Coping, and Healing After the Sudden Death of a Loved One*. Champion Press, Fox Point, Wisconsin, 2000.

Peck, M. Scott. *People of the Lie: The Hope for Healing Human Evil*. Simon and Schuster, New York, New York, 1997.

Reeve, Christopher. *Still Me*. Random, New York, New York, 1999.

Remen, Rachel Naomi. *Kitchen Table Wisdom: Stories That Heal*. Berkeley Publishing, New York, New York, 1997.

Schuller, Robert H. *Tough Times Never Last Forever, but Tough People Do*. Bantam Books, New York, New York, 1984.

Seligman, Martin E. P. *Learned Optimism*. Alfred A. Knopf, New York, New York, 1991.

Siebert, Al. *The Survivor Personality: Why Some People Are Stronger, Smarter, and More Skillful at Handling Life's Difficulties . . . and How You Can Be, Too*. Berkeley, New York, New York, 1996.